www.wadsworth.com

wadsworth.com is the World Wide Web site for Wadsworth Publishing Company and is your direct source to dozens of online resources.

At *wadsworth.com* you can find out about supplements, demonstration software, and student resources. You can also send e-mail to many of our authors and preview new publications and exciting new technologies.

wadsworth.com
Changing the way the world learns®

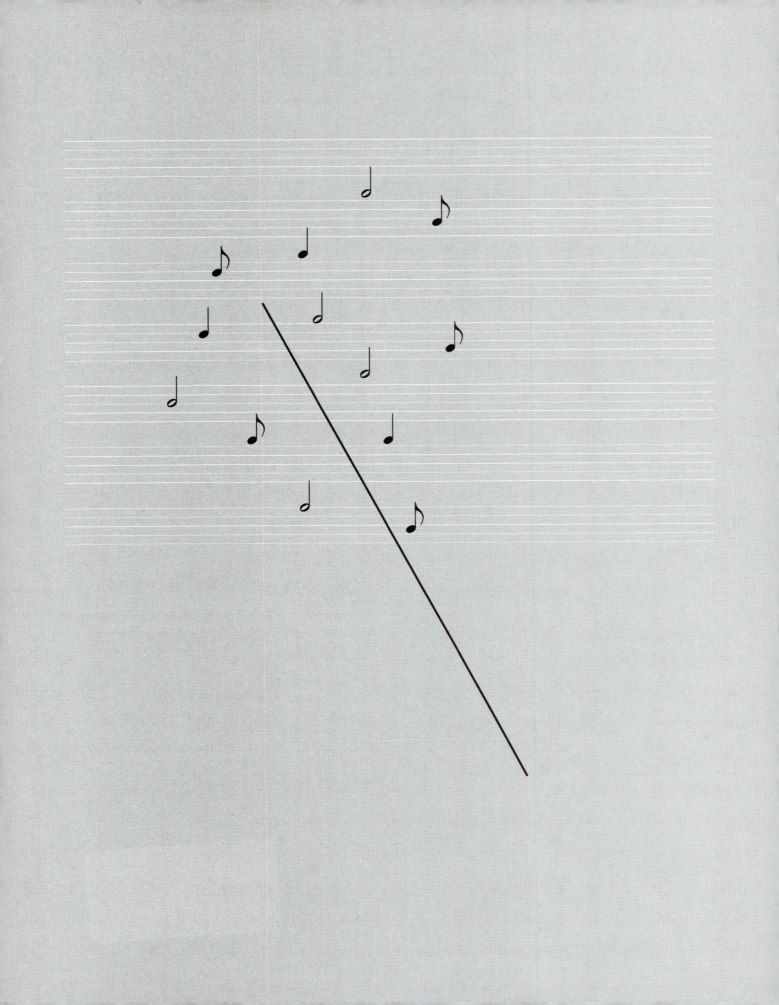

A Conducting Workbook

with CD-ROM Video

William Shepherd

University of Northern Iowa

SCHIRMER

THOMSON LEARNING

Australia • Canada • Mexico • Singapore • Spain
United Kingdom • United States

SCHIRMER

THOMSON LEARNING

Music Publisher: Clark Baxter
Development Editor: Abigail Baxter
Assistant Editor: Julie Iannacchino
Editorial Assistant: Jon Katz
Technology Project Manager: Steve Wainwright
Marketing Manager: Mark Orr
Marketing Assistant: Justine Ferguson
Advertising Project Manager: Brian Chaffee
Project Manager, Editorial Production: Teri Hyde
Print/Media Buyer: Tandra Jorgensen

Production Service: Johnstone Associates
Text Designer: Harry Voigt
Illustrator: Ray Gloor
Autographer: Mansfield Music-Graphics
Cover Designer: Cuttriss & Hambleton
Cover Image: © 2001 Eric Pearle/FPG International/LLC
Cover Printer: Malloy Lithographing, Inc.
Compositor: TBH Typecast, Inc.
Printer: Malloy Lithographing, Inc.

Printed in the United States of America
1 2 3 4 5 6 06 05 04 03 02 01

ISBN 0-534-52896-1

For permission to use material from this text, contact us by:
Web: http://www.thomsonrights.com
Fax: 1-800-730-2215
Phone: 1-800-730-2214

Wadsworth Group/Thomson Learning
10 Davis Drive
Belmont, CA 94002-3098
USA

For more information about our products, contact us:
Thomson Learning Academic Resource Center
1-800-423-0563
http://www.wadsworth.com

International Headquarters
Thomson Learning
International Division
290 Harbor Drive, 2nd Floor
Stamford, CT 06902-7477
USA

UK/Europe/Middle East/South Africa
Thomson Learning
Berkshire House
168–173 High Holborn
London WC1V 7AA
United Kingdom

Asia
Thomson Learning
60 Albert Street, #15-01
Albert Complex
Singapore 189969

Canada
Nelson Thomson Learning
1120 Birchmount Road
Toronto, Ontario M1K 5G4
Canada

To my parents, Bill and Helen Shepherd,
for making my life possible, and for their
unconditional love, support, and encouragement.

To my children, Ann, Jean, Nola, and Will,
for making my life worth living.

To all the students whose lives have touched mine.

Contents

Foreword

This book is an excellent guide for the beginning or intermediate conductor. It is written concisely and offers numerous examples of what you may encounter in your studies and experience as a conductor. Used properly, it will act as a resource as you confront conducting problems in years to come.

I have been conducting professionally for the last twenty-five years. In that time I have had the privilege of working with thousands of musicians of all ages—from junior high intermediate orchestras to the Chicago Symphony and London Philharmonic. Common to these varied experiences is the expectations of the musicians that the conductor will have a clean and secure technique. Musicians expect rhythmic precision, musical integrity, proper cuing and enunciation, a keen ear, and, most important, inspiration. Ultimately, you don't want to worry about technique but only about shaping the overall musical form so that you can reunite your musicians with the composer's intentions.

This takes a lifetime of study, discipline, and practice. None of us ever feels that we have enough time on the podium. There is no replacement for the sounds that come back to your ear. Your mind digests them and you begin to evaluate what's right or wrong about those sounds. However, there is no reason why a young conductor cannot study and understand the intentions of every composer and develop a clear, concise technique to back up those intentions. If you are able to accomplish this, you will be a successful and inspiring conductor. This book will give you enough information on the technical aspects. The rest is up to you—and it may well be the biggest challenge of your life.

Joseph Giunta
Music Director and Conductor
Des Moines Symphony Orchestra

Making the Transition from Performer to Conductor

An early challenge for the young conductor is to make the mental, physical, and emotional transition from performer to conductor. As a performer you are asked to balance, blend, play in tune, and contribute to the ensemble. You subordinate your playing to the overall sound of the ensemble and your focus tends to be individual or sectional. The conductor, on the other hand, focuses on the entire ensemble, solving problems and making decisions from the podium in a matter of seconds.

Generally, by the time you begin the study of conducting, you have been practicing and playing an instrument for several years. The temptation to take shortcuts in the study of conducting will be very strong. Try to remember that conducting requires the same study and practice as any musical discipline.

You will need to approach the study of conducting with the same dedication and diligence that you devoted to the study of your instrument. Just as you studied scales, études, solos, rudiments, and clefs in an effort to master your instrument, you will need to study carefully the exercises in this book if you are to become a musical and precise conductor. Would you go to your applied lesson without practicing? Practice the basics of conducting with the same intensity you practice your instrument.

Treat the conducting class as if it were your ensemble and assume the responsibilities of a conductor. This means that you should arrive before the class/rehearsal starts to make sure you and the rehearsal room are prepared. There is no excuse for the conductor to be unprepared; the unprepared conductor wastes the time of every member in the ensemble. Furthermore, you must demand promptness and attendance from your ensemble. Unless there is a serious illness or other extreme circumstance, never miss a class/rehearsal.

Personality

As strange as it may seem as a beginning conductor, your personality will emerge through the end of your baton. Just as you project your personality through your instrument you will project as a conductor.

Be true to yourself and your musical values. Do not be afraid to allow those you are conducting to see your true self. Accept only the best from your musicians—never second best.

Diversity of personality is one of the wonderful facets of conducting. Each personality and musical background contributes to making each conductor's musical interpretations different from another's. Thus it is essential that each conductor have a basic vocabulary of technique and knowledge to allow musicianship, individuality, and personality to become effective.

The Qualities of a Good Conductor

- Possesses excellent musicianship
- Knows music history and the correct interpretation of styles and musical periods
- Understands how to balance music within each section and between sections
- Understands all transpositions
- Knows fingerings and positions for all instruments and the technical difficulties associated with each instrument
- Identifies, understands, and solves pitch problems inherent to each instrument
- Discriminates and corrects rhythm problems
- Knows performers' abilities and personalities
- Conducts the ensemble in performance as conducted in rehearsal
- Possesses integrity
- Loves music
- Motivates and inspires

Using the Text

This text accommodates a variety of learning situations, from one teacher–one student to one teacher and a nearly unlimited number of students per class. If there is only one student and one teacher, the teacher may play the exercises while the student conducts. If the class is larger, class members should act as the ensemble. The exercises require each student to practice with a metronome.

Many of the exercises have more conducting challenges than would normally be found in such short musical segments; this is especially true of the exercises with fermati. You will encounter all of these challenges, however, in actual conducting. If you are able to master the exercises that follow, you will have gained solid grounding in the basics of conducting.

Developing a fine conducting technique—one that gives musicians a clear, inspiring, concise beat pattern—is only the first and most important step in becoming a conductor. When you have mastered conducting, rehearsal, and score-study techniques, and then infused technique with your own musicality, you will be well on your way toward becoming a truly musical conductor.

Additional Material on the Wadsworth Web Site

For those readers who are interested in pursuing further knowledge and practice, please note that the World Wide Web icons found in this text relate to additional material located on this book's Web site at *http://www.wadsworth.com/music.*

Using the Basic Conducting CD

Introduction

This interactive program was developed to enhance visually the information found in this workbook. The CD has been developed to run on both Windows and Macintosh platforms. In the following you will find information regarding system requirements. You will also find directions for both PC and Macintosh users on how to use this interactive program as well as on how to install QuickTime.

Windows System Requirements

- Windows 95, Windows 98, Windows NT, and Windows 2000
- Intel Pentium or compatible processor
- 16 MB of RAM
- Sound Blaster or compatible sound card and speakers
- DirectX version 3.0 or later is recommended

Macintosh System Requirements

- Power PC CPU or later
- Mac OS version 7.5.5 or higher
- Open Transport version 1.2 or higher
- At least 16 MB of RAM

Using this CD with Macintosh

1. Once the CD has started running, you will be shown an opening screen that asks you to push the start button to begin using the program. It will also remind you that you must have QuickTime 3 (or higher) installed on your computer.

2. *If you do not have QuickTime installed, please quit the program by clicking in the upper left-hand corner of the program window. Directions on how to load QuickTime are found below.*

3. If QuickTime is properly installed, click start. That will take you to the main menu of the program. Here, you may choose the chapter you would like to view by clicking on the corresponding number found along the top of the screen.

4. Once you have chosen the chapter you want, you may then choose the specific video you want to view. The video titles are listed under the chapter heading. Click on the title you would like to view.

5. A black box will appear in the left portion of the Conductor screen. The lower portion of the black box has a controller bar. This bar allows you to start playing the video, stop it, adjust the volume, as well as fast forward and rewind. When you place your pointer over these controls a balloon will appear telling you what its specific function is (you must have the Show Balloons function on; it is found under the Help menu).

6. You may also navigate through the program by using the arrow buttons. These arrows will allow you to go one step forward or backward. To quit the program, click on the small box in the upper left-hand corner of the Conductor screen. Enjoy!

Installing QuickTime / Macintosh

Here are the instructions for installing the *QuickTime Player* that is provided on this CD. The same instructions are found in the Conductor folder.

1. Double click on the *QuickTime Installer* icon found in the Conductor CD folder. It is next to the Conductor icon. This folder should automatically be open and on your desktop when you are using the Conductor CD.

2. Once the installer opens you will be greeted with a *Welcome* screen. Press the Next button at the bottom of the dialogue box.

3. The following screen will remind you to quit all other programs you may have running. If you do not have any programs running, press *Next*. If you do have programs running, you will need to exit the program to close them and then start the installation program again.

4. You will then be presented with a licensing agreement. Please read it completely and then click *Next*.

5. You will now be asked to choose an installation type. Choose minimum. This is the best choice and will take the least amount of time to install. Click *Next*.

6. You will now be at the registration screen. Fill in your name and organization (if it applies). You are not required to fill out the registration number. Press *Next*.

7. You will now be asked to make sure you are connected to the Internet. When you have verified that you have a connection, then click *Next*. Your computer will now install the required files.

8. When the download process is complete you will be asked if you want to continue with other installations or quit. Press *Next*.

9. You will now see an open folder that shows you files you have loaded onto your computer. Please take a moment to identify these files, then close the folder. You are now finished with the installation process. You will be asked to restart your computer. Once you have done so you are ready to start using The Conductor program.

Using this CD with a PC

1. This program should start running automatically once inserted into your computer's CD-ROM drive.

2. If you have *auto play* disabled on your computer, the CD-ROM will not start automatically. In order to start the program, double click on *My Computer* on the desktop, then right click on your CD-ROM player icon and choose *explore* from the shortcut menu.

3. By doing this, you will be able to locate all of the files on this CD. Double click on the icon entitled *Conduct.exe*. This will launch the program for you.

4. Once the CD has started running, you will be shown an opening screen that will ask you to push the start button to begin using the program. It will also remind you that you must have *QuickTime 3* (or higher) installed on your computer.

5. If you do not have QuickTime installed, please quit the program by clicking the X in the upper right-hand corner of the program window. Directions on how to load QuickTime are found below.

6. *If QuickTime is properly installed, click start. That will take you to the program's main menu. Here, you may choose the chapter you would like to view by clicking on the corresponding number found along the top of the screen.*

7. Once you have chosen the chapter you want, you may then choose the specific video you want to view. The video titles are listed under the chapter heading. Click on the title you want.

8. You will notice that a black box appears in the left portion of the Conductor screen. The lower portion of the black box has a controller bar. This bar will allow you to start playing the video, stop it, adjust the volume, as well as fast forward and rewind.

9. You may also navigate through the program by using the arrow buttons. These arrows will allow you to go one step forward or backward. To quite the program, click on the X in the upper right-hand corner of the program window. Enjoy!

Installing QuickTime / PC

Follow these instructions to install the QuickTime Player provided on this CD.

1. **Windows 95/98 and Windows NT:** Go to *My Computer* on the desktop, then right click on your CD-ROM player icon and choose *explore* from the shortcut menu. By doing this you will be able to locate all of the files on this CD.

2. Double click on the folder entitled Qt4. Then double click on the icon entitled *Quicktime.exe*. This will launch the QuickTime installer program for you.

3. When the installer opens you will be greeted with a *welcome* screen. Press the Next button at the bottom of the dialogue box.

4. This screen will remind you to quit all other programs you may have running. If you do not have any programs running, press *Next*. If you do, you will need to exit the install program to close them and then start the installation program again.

5. The next screen is a licensing ageement. Please read it completely and then click *Next* if you agree to the terms.

6. You must now identify the destination directory for QuickTime. Once you have done so, click *Next*.

7. Choose minimum as the installation type. This is the best choice and will take the least amount of time to install. Click *Next*.

8. You will now be asked to verify and/or change the name of the Program Folder where QuickTime will be placed. Once you do so, click *Next*.

9. The next screen will ask you about installing QuickTime plug-in options for Netscape and Microsoft Internet Explorer. Choose which browser(s) you would like to install plug-ins for and click *Next*.

10. You will now be at the registration screen. Fill in your name and organization (if it applies). You are not required to fill out the registration number. Then press *Next*.

11. When the download process is complete, you will be asked if you want to continue with other installations or quit. Press *Quit*.

12. You will now see an open folder that shows you files you have loaded onto your machine. Please take a moment to identify these files. Once you are finished viewing the files, close the folder. You are now done with the installation process. Enjoy!

Acknowledgments

Thank you to the following who gave their time in interviews to discuss the world of conducting.

Richard Clary
The University of Kentucky
Lexington, KY 40292

Harry Clarke, Head
The University of Kentucky
Lexington, KY 40506

Michael Fanelli
Price Lab School
Cedar Falls, IA 50613

Janelle French
Summes Hill
Muswellbrook NSW 2333
Australia

Maestro Joseph Giunta
Des Moines Symphony Orchestra
Des Moines, IA

Karl Holvik, Emeritus
University of Northern Iowa
Cedar Falls, IA 50614

Bob Hower
Adelaide University
Adelaide, Australia

Ralph Hultgren
Queensland University
Brisbane, Australia

Ronald Johnson
University of Northern Iowa
Cedar Falls, IA 50614

Esther McGuire
Waterloo Public Schools
Waterloo, IA 50701

William McGuire
Professional Organist/Conductor
Waterloo, IA 50701

Monte Mumford
University of Tasmania
Tasmania, Australia

Acton Ostling, Jr.
University of Louisville
Louisville, KY 40292

Russell W. Passfield
68 Shiraz St
Muswellbrook NSW 2333
Australia

Jeffrey Renshaw
University of Connecticut
Storrs, CT 06269

John Vallentine
University of Northern Iowa
Cedar Falls, IA 50614

Steve Williams
New South Wales University
Sydney, Australia

Credits

Thank you to the following who shared their talent to help me create this program for you:

Joe Marchesani	*Video tape filming and directing*
John Mathias	*Video tape editing*
Elaine Wong	*Clarinet*
Kathleen Sander	*Flute*
Darrell Fremont	*Video disk preparing and producing*
Tom C. Peterson	*PowerPoint program assembling*
Justin Stone	*Project producer and designer*
Esther McGuire	*PowerPoint program editing*
Bill McGuire	*Preparation of Bach chorales*
Jason McGovern	*Post production and distribution*

CHAPTER 1

Basics of Conducting

Batons

Some conductors spend considerable time and effort selecting just the right baton. An experienced conductor, however, soon realizes that the person holding the baton is infinitely more important than the baton.

Within reason and comfort, the baton should be an extension of the forearm and wrist. Depending on the size of the conductor's hand and physical makeup and, to a degree, the ensemble being conducted, the baton should feel comfortable when held between the thumb and first knuckle of the forefinger with the handle of the baton resting against the fleshy heel of the hand.

The length of the baton is also a matter of personal preference. One simple test for length is to rest the handle of the baton in the crook of the elbow with the tip of the baton extending just beyond the fingertips.

Balance of the baton may be determined by holding the baton between the thumb and forefinger or by actually balancing the baton on the forefinger.

The purpose of the baton is to give greater clarity to your conducting patterns. The tip of the baton should outline a clear, easy-to-read pattern. Focus the conducting pattern at the tip of the baton.

The true tests of a baton are if you can answer yes to the following questions:

- Does the baton feel comfortable in your hand?
- Does the baton enhance your conducting and musical communication?

Posture

Good posture is extremely important while conducting. Not only will you be more comfortable conducting and rehearsing but good posture also sends a signal to your ensemble that you are prepared, confident, knowledgeable, and able to lead them musically, artistically, and technically. Poor posture, on the other hand, sends a signal to your ensemble that you are less than enthusiastic about the music and the musicians.

People of small stature will appear tall if they have good posture and a positive attitude. A person with sagging shoulders and an unhappy expression will be an ineffective conductor. The issue of body language is too complex to deal with in this text, but further study of body language will be extremely helpful to the conductor and to those being conducted.

Your feet should be a comfortable distance apart for good balance. One foot will usually be slightly ahead of the other. A conductor who is right-footed usually places the right foot ahead, while the left-footed conductor places the left foot slightly ahead.

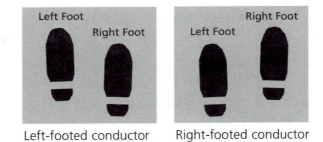

Left-footed conductor   Right-footed conductor

Your shoulders should be relaxed, not slumped, to avoid fatigue during a long rehearsal. The entire body should be relaxed enough to allow the conductor to express the music without undue tension. Your face should reflect what the music demands. A smiling face would be appropriate for a Sousa march, while a solemn look would be more appropriate for the opening chord of Frescobaldi's *Toccata*.

Exercise 1.1   First Sounds on the Podium

Objective: Become accustomed to hearing sound from the ensemble while on the podium.

Each person should conduct the class using a scale of his or her own choosing. To permit maximal aural perception and maximal eye contact, remove the music stand between the conductor and the class.

1. Conduct the scale at ♩ = 80 MM, one scale step per measure and one count per note. Example: four B♭ quarter notes in the first measure. Start with $\frac{4}{4}$ time, then practice using additional time signatures and scales.

2. As you conduct the scale, close your eyes in alternate measures to be free of external distractions and concentrate on the sound.

Exercise 1.2   Mobility

Objective: Foster mobility and good posture on the podium by keeping the body relaxed.

Use a metronome (♩ = 96–130) and practice these exercises without an ensemble in $\frac{2}{4}$, $\frac{3}{4}$, $\frac{4}{4}$, and $\frac{5}{4}$ time.

1. After choosing the time signature and tempo, conduct four measures, make a quarter turn to the right, conduct four measures, make a quarter turn to the right, conduct four measures, make a quarter turn to the

right, conduct four measures, make a quarter turn to the right, conduct four measures. Repeat using other time signatures and tempi.

2. After choosing the time signature and tempo, conduct four measures, make a quarter turn to the left, conduct four measures, make a quarter turn to the left, conduct four measures, make a quarter turn to the left, conduct four measures, make a quarter turn to the left, conduct four measures. Repeat using other time signatures and tempi.

3. After choosing the time signature and tempo, conduct four measures, take one step forward, conduct four measures, take one step backward, conduct four measures, take one step to the right, conduct four measures, take one step to the left, conduct four measures. Repeat using other time signatures and tempi.

4. Use different combinations of movements, time signatures, and tempi.

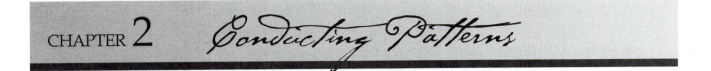
Terms Used in the Conducting Pattern

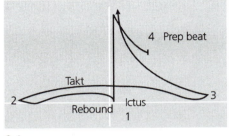

2.1

1. *Prep beat.* Gives players time to breathe and prepare to start the sound. The prep beat should show the musicians the

   ■ Tempo of the composition

   ■ Volume of the entrance

   ■ Style of the composition

2. *Ictus.* The point at which the sound begins.

3. *Takt.* The path and distance the baton travels from one ictus point to the next.

4. *Rebound.* The natural upward movement after the ictus has been conducted.

Exercise 2.1   ***Hinged-Wrist Motion***

Objective: Achieve the proper hinged-wrist motion.

Conduct pattern with and without a metronome.

1. Practice without the baton to achieve the hinged-wrist motion that avoids a stiff, unmusical pattern.

2. Use the baton with the same hinged-wrist action.

Patterns

Make your conducting patterns look as much as possible like the following diagrams.

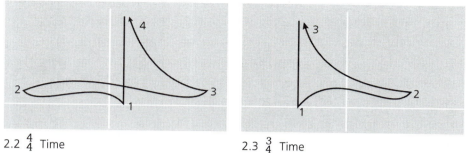

2.2 $\frac{4}{4}$ Time

2.3 $\frac{3}{4}$ Time

2.4 $\frac{3}{4}$ Time in 1

2.5 $\frac{2}{4}$ Time, Loop Pattern

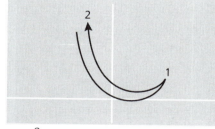

2.6 $\frac{2}{4}$ Time, Fishhook Pattern

2.7 $\frac{2}{4}$ Time in One Pattern

To prepare for conducting a two pattern in one, practice the following. Conduct beat 1 straight down, beat 2 straight up. Use a quick flick of the wrist for each motion.

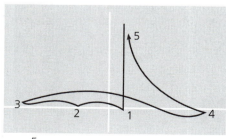

2.8 $\frac{5}{4}$ Time (3 + 2)

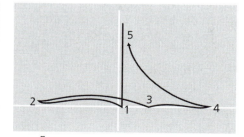

2.9 $\frac{5}{4}$ Time (2 + 3)

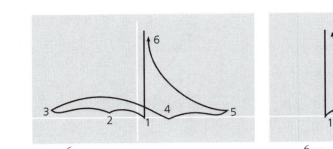

2.10 ⁶⁄₈ Time   2.11 ⁶⁄₈ Time

Exercise 2.2   *Stamina*

Objectives: (1) Gain familiarity and reach a comfort level conducting basic patterns, and (2) concentrate on the mechanics of a specific conducting pattern.

Using a variety of conducting patterns and tempi, the instructor will set the metronome to a specific tempo and select a conducting pattern.

1. Conduct a specific pattern from the above diagrams, without a baton, until you are tired. Initially, this will happen quickly, but your stamina will increase with practice. Meanwhile, this exercise will help you to understand the necessity of using precise patterns. Remember to relax while conducting.

2. Be mindful of your hand positions, posture, conducting patterns, and overall demeanor.

The Prep Beat

Exercise 2.3   *Prep Beat Preparation*

Objective: Use the correct prep beat.

1. Find the correct prep beat by conducting the basic pattern indicated in the time signature of the example.

2. Give only *one* movement for each preparation beat.

3. Conduct, in tempo, to the last beat of the measure that contains a fermata. On the last beat, extend the measure by at least half the value of the measure. Release the fermata by making a loop that ends to the right—as in the following diagram. (See also Diagram 3.13, ⁴⁄₄ time, count 4, in Chapter 3.)

4. Come to a complete stop after each example.

5. For examples 1–9, set your metronome at ♩ = 88–120.

6. For examples 10–15, set your metronome at ♪ = 88–120 (in six, not two).

Exercise 2.3

Treble Part

Exercise 2.3

F Part

Exercise 2.3

E♭ Part

Exercise 2.3

B♭ Part

Exercise 2.3

Bass Part

Prep Beat Preparation

Exercise 2.4

Objective: Use the correct preparation beat.

1. Find the correct prep beat by conducting the basic pattern indicated in the time signature of the example.

2. Give only *one* movement for each prep beat.

3. Show the prep beat by giving a *sharp ictus* on the eighth rest, then allow the baton hand to rebound as the eighth note is played.

4. Conduct, in tempo, to the last beat of measure that contains a fermata. On the last beat, extend the measure by at least half the value of the measure. Release the fermata by making a loop that ends to the right— as in the following diagram. (See also 4/4 Time count 4 in Chapter 3.)

5. Come to a complete stop after each example.

6. For Examples 1–9, set your metronome ♩ = 88–120.

7. For Examples 10–15, set your metronome at ♪ = 88–120 (in six, not two).

Exercise 2.4

Treble Part

F Part

Exercise 2.4

E♭ Part

Exercise 2.4

B♭ Part

Exercise 2.4

Bass Part

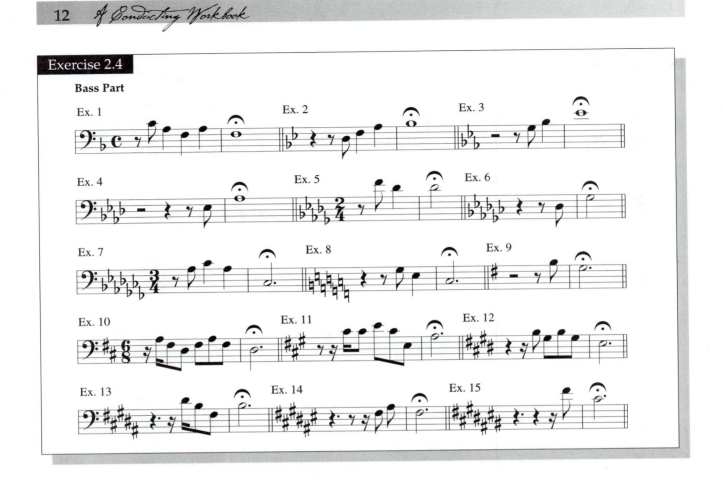

Exercise 2.5   *Mobility*

Conduct Exercises 2.3 and 2.4 with a one-measure rest after each exercise (♩ = 60–120).

Exercise 2.6   *Patterns and Prep Beats*

Conduct each pattern twice, take one count rest, then move to the next pattern with prep (♩ = 60–120).

CHAPTER 3   *Fermati*

Fermati Release Conducting Patterns

*C*onductors consistently encounter difficult musical problems with fermati. Practicing the following exercises will help prepare you to use the proper release from a fermata.

After you release a fermata, the baton must be in the correct position to give the preparation beat for the next entrance. If you have a question about the proper release direction and the following preparation beat, rethink the basic pattern you are conducting and you will find the answer.

A word about conducting the last note of a phrase (if there is space after the phrase) or the last note of a composition that does not include a fermata: If the release is given on the last note, the note will be played short. If the note needs to be played full-value, the note should be released on the following beat. Frequently, the last note of most phrases or compositions is played too short.

Fermati Release   *Exercise 3.1*

Objective: Train the mind and muscles to release in the correct direction from any fermata.

1. Come to a complete stop after each release.

2. After you have completed a release, you must be in position to give the correct prep beat for the new entrance (unless you are at the end of a composition).

3. Using the same format of releases, practice in $\frac{2}{4}$, $\frac{3}{4}$, $\frac{5}{4}$, and $\frac{6}{8}$ time.

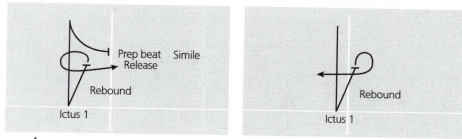

3.1 $\frac{4}{4}$ Time, Count 1   3.2 $\frac{4}{4}$ Time, Count 1

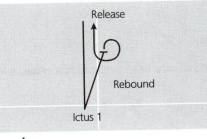

3.3 $\frac{4}{4}$ Time, Count 1

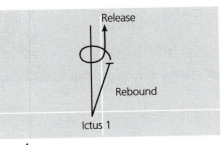

3.4 $\frac{4}{4}$ Time, Count 1

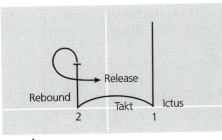

3.5 $\frac{4}{4}$ Time, Count 2

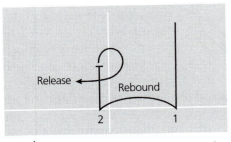

3.6 $\frac{4}{4}$ Time, Count 2

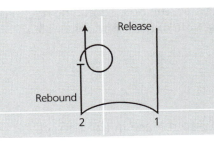

3.7 $\frac{4}{4}$ Time, Count 2

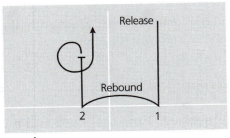

3.8 $\frac{4}{4}$ Time, Count 2

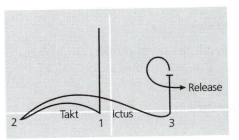

3.9 $\frac{4}{4}$ Time, Count 3

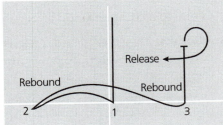

3.10 $\frac{4}{4}$ Time, Count 3

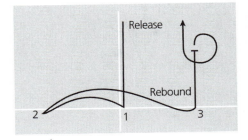

3.11 $\frac{4}{4}$ Time, Count 3

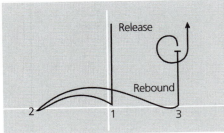

3.12 $\frac{4}{4}$ Time, Count 3

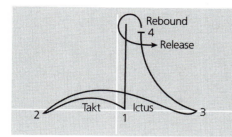

3.13 $\frac{4}{4}$ Time, Count 4

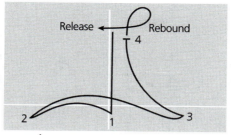

3.14 $\frac{4}{4}$ Time, Count 4

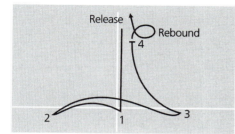

3.15 $\frac{4}{4}$ Time, Count 4

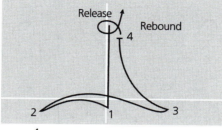

3.16 $\frac{4}{4}$ Time, Count 4

Directional Release for Fermati

Fermati Release   *Exercise 3.2*

Objective: Use the correct directional release that will lead to the correct preparation beat of the next entrance after a fermata.

1. After using a prep beat and conducting the downbeat of the following example, allow the baton hand to rise, then release the fermata with a loop to the left and up, coming to a complete stop.

This motion will position you to re-conduct beat one, which is the prep beat for the entrance on two. (Refer also to Diagrams 3.3 and 3.4 on page 14 because they each show the same release but from different sides of the downstroke.)

2. Use only *one motion* for *each* prep beat.

3. Conduct all beats in the second measure of each example.

4. Repeat the same procedure for all the examples.

Exercise 3.2

Treble Part

Exercise 3.2

F Part

Exercise 3.2

E♭ Part

Exercise 3.2

B♭ Part

Exercise 3.2

Bass Part

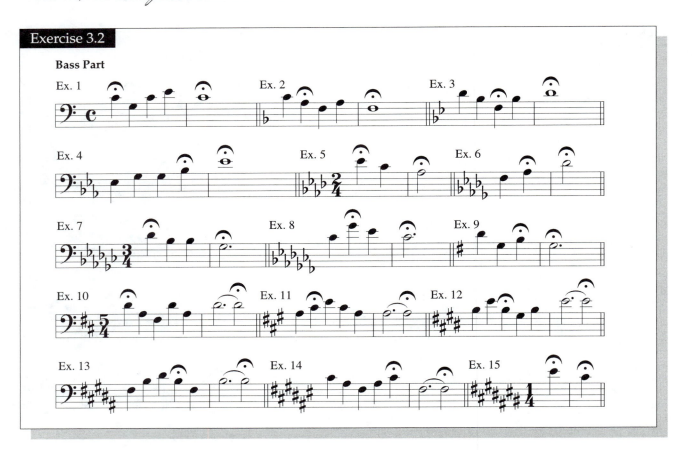

Exercise 3.3 *Fermati Release and Prep Beat*

Objective: Use the correct directional release that will lead to the correct prep beat of the next entrance after a fermata ($\quarternote$ = 80–132).

For the *full ensemble:*

1. Conduct each example with a caesura after each fermata. The baton should come to a complete stop after the release of each fermata.

2. Conduct each example without a caesura after each fermata.

3. Select any major or minor scale and play a different scale step on each measure.

For the *individual parts:*

1. Conduct each example with a caesura after each fermata. The baton should come to a complete stop after the release of each fermata.

2. Conduct each example without a caesura after each fermata.

Exercise 3.3

Ensemble

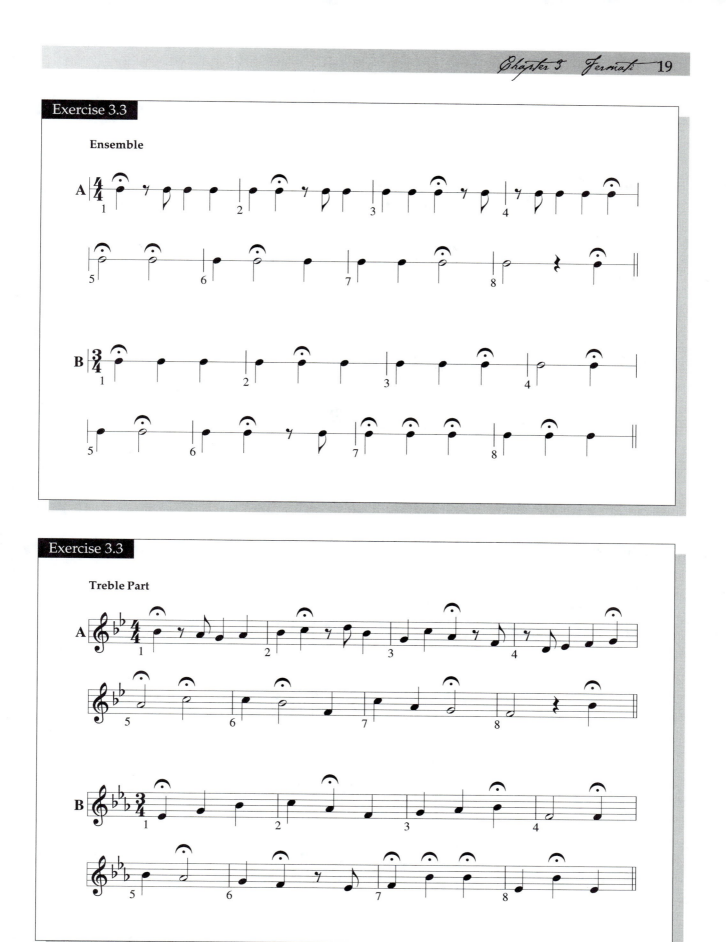

Exercise 3.3

Treble Part

Exercise 3.3

F Part

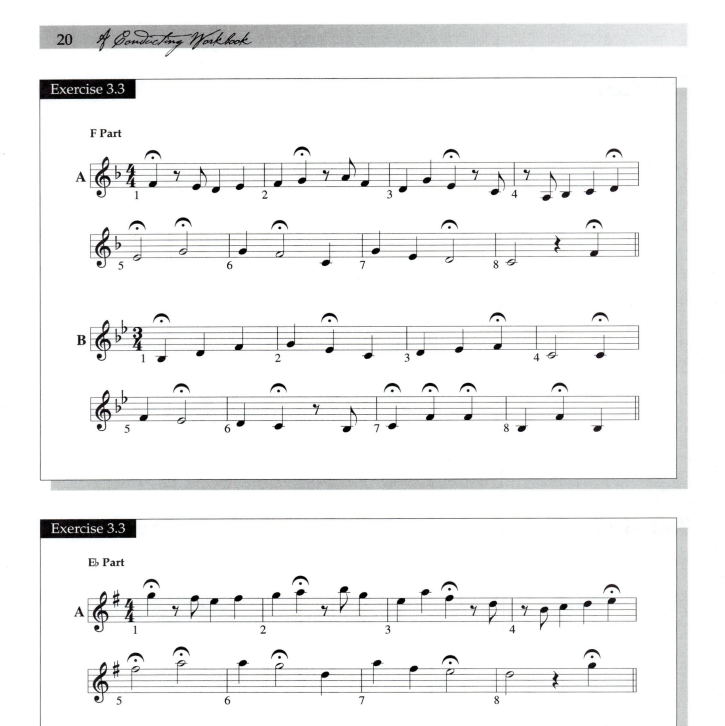

Exercise 3.3

E♭ Part

Exercise 3.3

B♭ Part

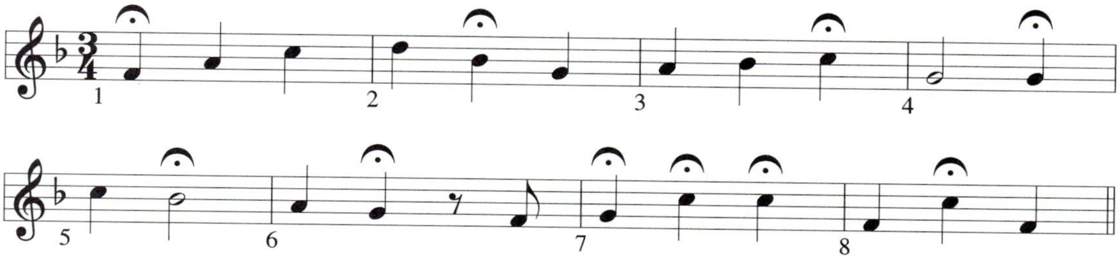

Exercise 3.3

Bass Part

Prep Beats and Fermati

Exercise 3.4   *Fermati Release and Prep Beat*

For this exercise, use ♩ = 60–120.

1. Using the conducting patterns in Chapter 2, hold each fermata an additional two counts.
2. Release on the next count.
3. Rest two counts, then give the prep beat for the next entrance.

Exercise 3.5   *Fermati Release and Prep Beat*

For this exercise, use ♩ = 60 *a piacere.* Using the music examples in Exercise 3.2, conduct

- One-count prep beat
- Two counts for a quarter note with a fermata
- One-count release
- One-count rest
- One-count new prep beat
- Give the second measure of each exercise two additional counts and one count release.
- Rest two counts.
- Initiate prep beat for the next exercise.

Exercise 3.6   *Fermati Release and Prep Beat*

For this exercise, use ♩ = 60–120. Using the music examples in Exercise 3.3, conduct

- One-count prep beat
- Two counts for a quarter note with a fermata
- One-count release
- One-count rest
- One-count new prep
- Give each half-note three counts.
- One-count release
- Rest one count.
- Initiate one-count prep beat.

Luftpause, a third type of fermata, may be viewed and downloaded at *http://www.wadsworth.com/music.*

CHAPTER 4 — Left-Hand Cuing

Make a fist with your left hand. Maintaining your left hand in a fist, extend the left forefinger. There are, of course, other hand positions and ways of giving cues, but we will begin with this configuration. Do not push your finger straight toward players or cue them as if you were shooting a pistol; use the forefinger as if it were a small baton. When giving a cue on the beat, think of showing an ictus with the forefinger, much the same as giving a downbeat ictus with the baton in the right hand.

Practice left-hand cuing by locking your left elbow tightly against the left rib cage and moving the forearm up and down from the elbow with the forefinger extended. This motion will help focus your control of the cuing motion. When the motion is comfortable, move the left arm forward to a normal cuing position and give cues in a similar fashion.

In cuing an upbeat, entrance speed will determine how the left-hand cue is used. If the tempo is slow, the baton will show the ictus while the left hand cues directly on the upbeat. If the tempo is quick, the left hand will give the cue on the beat as a prep to play on the upbeat. Left-hand cues should match the dynamics, tempo, and style of the entrance being cued.

Other ways to cue players include eye contact, head motion, use of the right hand, and so on. For now, to gain greater left-hand/right-hand independence and coordination, use only the left hand for cuing.

Left-Hand Cuing with Metronome Only

Left-Hand Cuing   *Exercise 4.1*

Objective: Develop facility in left-hand cuing.

1. Use a metronome for these exercises.

2. As each cue is given, say the syllable *tah*.

3. Repeat exercises 1–30 until mastered.

For the following exercises, set the metronome at ♩ = 96–120.

4.1.1   Conduct a $\frac{4}{4}$ pattern and with the left-hand cue on 1.

4.1.2   Conduct a $\frac{4}{4}$ pattern and with the left-hand cue on 2.

4.1.3   Conduct a $\frac{4}{4}$ pattern and with the left-hand cue on 3.

4.1.4   Conduct a $\frac{4}{4}$ pattern and with the left-hand cue on 4.

4.1.5   Conduct a $\frac{4}{4}$ pattern and with the left-hand cue on 1 and 3.

4.1.6   Conduct a $\frac{4}{4}$ pattern and with the left-hand cue on 2 and 4.

4.1.7   Conduct a $\frac{4}{4}$ pattern and with the left-hand cue on 1 and 4.

4.1.8   Conduct a $\frac{3}{4}$ pattern and with the left-hand cue on 1.

4.1.9   Conduct a $\frac{3}{4}$ pattern and with the left-hand cue on 2.

4.1.10   Conduct a $\frac{3}{4}$ pattern and with the left-hand cue on 3.

4.1.11   Conduct a $\frac{3}{4}$ pattern and with the left-hand cue on 1 and 2.

4.1.12   Conduct a $\frac{3}{4}$ pattern and with the left-hand cue on 2 and 3.

4.1.13   Conduct a $\frac{3}{4}$ pattern and with the left-hand cue on 1 and 3.

4.1.14   Conduct a $\frac{2}{4}$ pattern and with the left-hand cue on 1.

4.1.15   Conduct a $\frac{2}{4}$ pattern and with the left-hand cue on 2.

4.1.16   Conduct a $\frac{2}{4}$ pattern and with the left-hand cue on 1.

For the following exercises, set your metronome at ♪ = 96–120.

4.1.17   Conduct a $\frac{6}{8}$ pattern and with the left-hand cue on 1.

4.1.18   Conduct a $\frac{6}{8}$ pattern and with the left-hand cue on 2.

4.1.19   Conduct a $\frac{6}{8}$ pattern and with the left-hand cue on 3.

4.1.20   Conduct a $\frac{6}{8}$ pattern and with the left-hand cue on 4.

4.1.21   Conduct a $\frac{6}{8}$ pattern and with the left-hand cue on 5.

4.1.22   Conduct a $\frac{6}{8}$ pattern and with the left-hand cue on 6.

4.1.23   Conduct a $\frac{6}{8}$ pattern and with the left-hand cue on 1 and 3.

4.1.24   Conduct a $\frac{6}{8}$ pattern and with the left-hand cue on 2 and 4.

4.1.25   Conduct a $\frac{6}{8}$ pattern and with the left-hand cue on 3 and 5.

4.1.26   Conduct a $\frac{6}{8}$ pattern and with the left-hand cue on 4 and 6.

4.1.27   Conduct a $\frac{6}{8}$ pattern and with the left-hand cue on 1, 3, and 5.

4.1.28   Conduct a $\frac{6}{8}$ pattern and with the left-hand cue on 2, 4, and 6.

4.1.29   Conduct a $\frac{6}{8}$ pattern and with the left-hand cue on 2, 4, 6, and 1.

4.1.30   Conduct all of the exercises again. This time cue the afterbeat of each entrance that you cued on the beat.

Left-Hand Cuing with Scales

Left-Hand Cuing   *Exercise 4.2*

This exercise may be used to conduct one player or the entire class as an ensemble.

1. After mastering all the cues of Exercise 4.1 without playing, the conductor chooses a scale to be played, one octave up and one down, continuously from 4.1.1 through 4.1.30.

2. Each cued note will be a new scale step.

3. The conductor should give all cues written in the exercise.

4. Players should not look at the printed page but watch the conductor.

5. Players should not play cued notes unless cued.

Left-Hand Cuing with Right-Hand Conducting

Left-Hand Cuing with Right-Hand Conducting   *Exercise 4.3*

Objective: Coordinate left-hand cuing with a right-hand conducting pattern.

1. Cue *every quarter note* with the left hand.

2. One half of the class plays the whole notes; the other half plays the quarter notes only if cued ($\quarternote$ = 72–120).

Exercise 4.3

Treble Part

Exercise 4.3

F Part

Exercise 4.3

E♭ Part

Exercise 4.3

Exercise 4.3

Bass Part

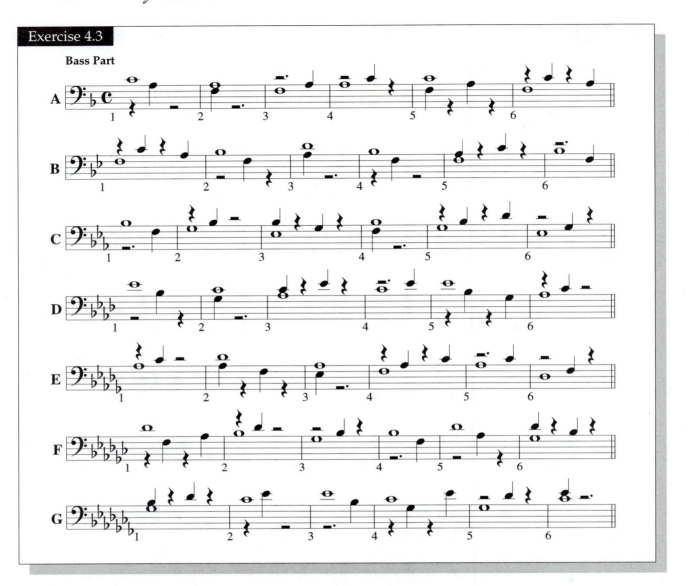

Left-Hand Cuing with Right-Hand Conducting

Exercise 4.4

Objective: Coordinate left-hand cuing with a right-hand conducting pattern.

1. Cue *every eighth note* with the left hand.

2. One half of the class plays the whole notes; the other half plays the quarter notes only if cued.

♩ = 72–120

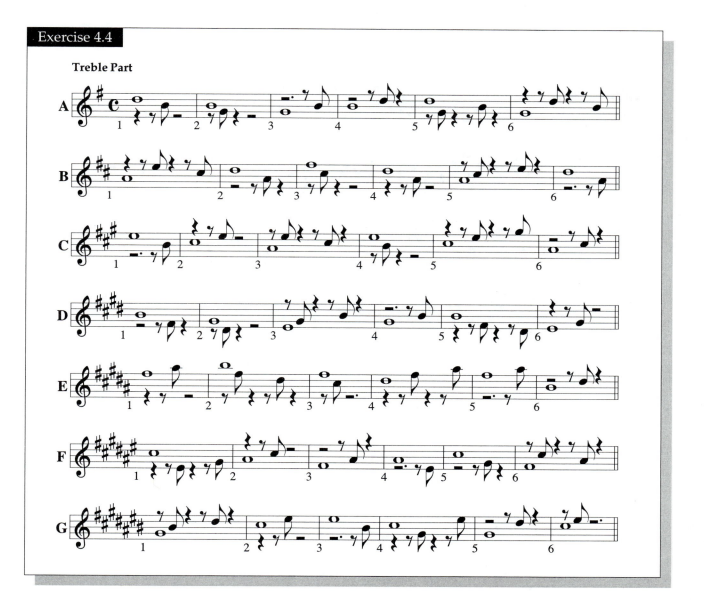

Exercise 4.4

F Part

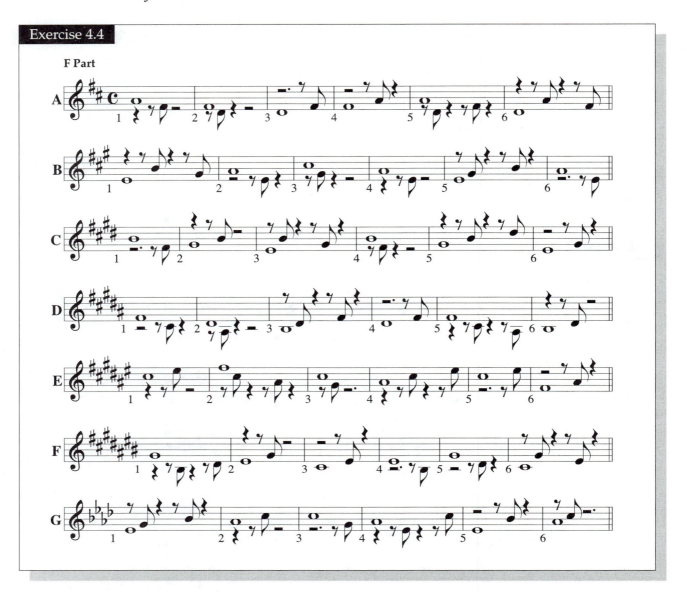

Exercise 4.4

Eb Part

Exercise 4.4

B♭ Part

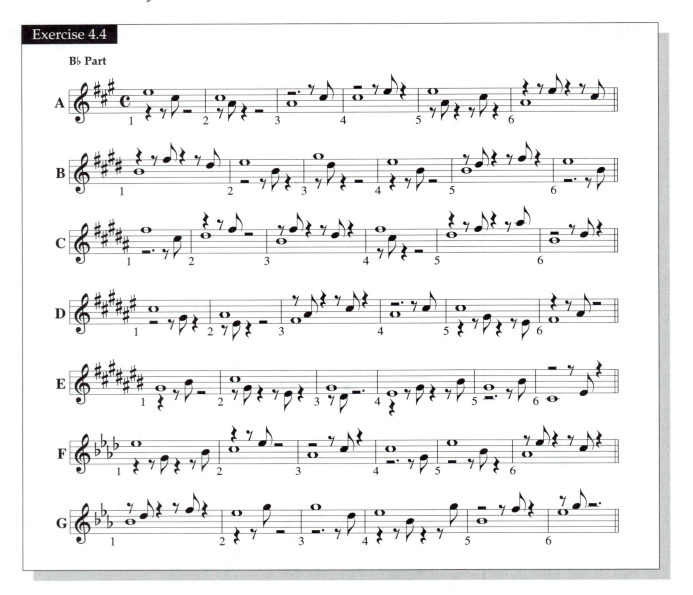

Exercise 4.4

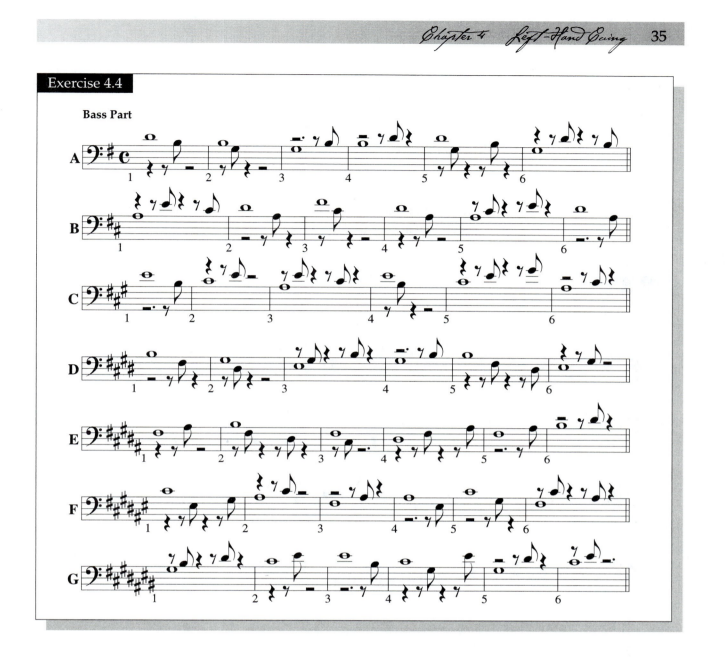

Exercise 4.5   Left-Hand Cuing with Right-Hand Conducting

Objective: Coordinate left-hand cuing with a right-hand conducting pattern.

1. Cue *every eighth note and quarter note* with the left hand.

2. One half of the class plays the lower notes; the other half plays the cued notes *only* if cued (♩ = 72–120).

Exercise 4.5

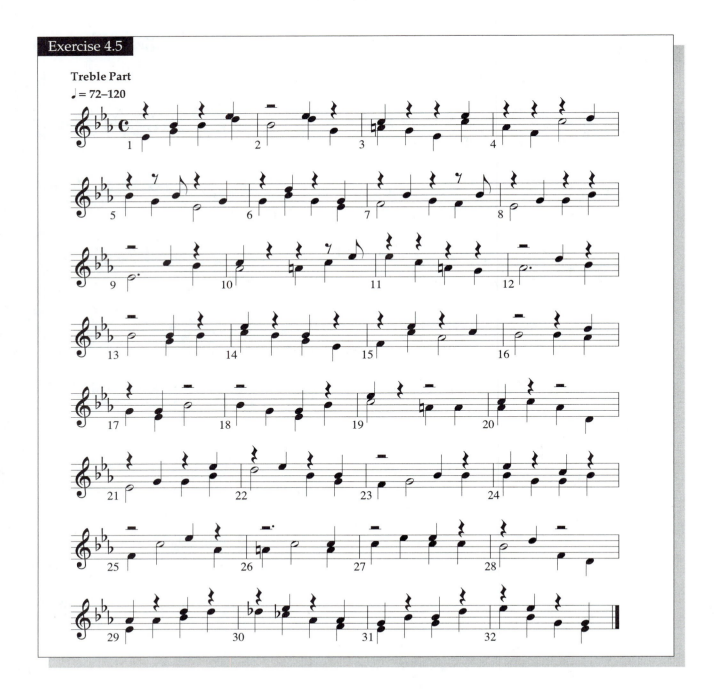

Exercise 4.5

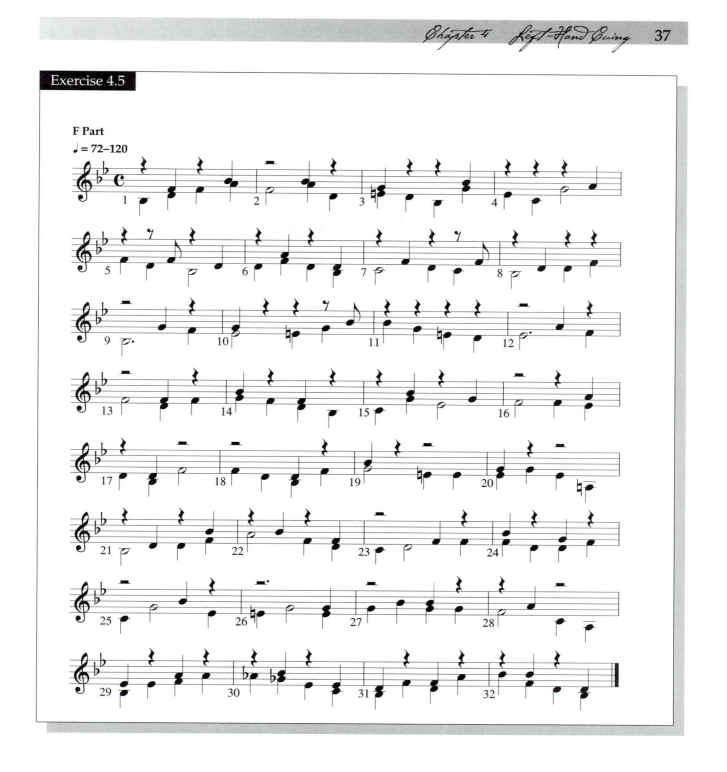

Exercise 4.5

E♭ Part

♩ = 72–120

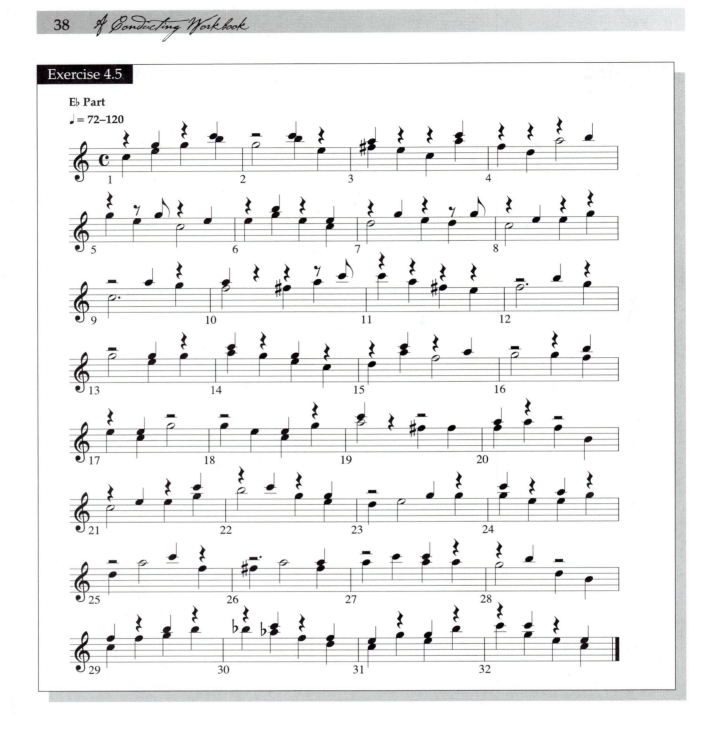

Exercise 4.5

B♭ Part

♩ = 72–120

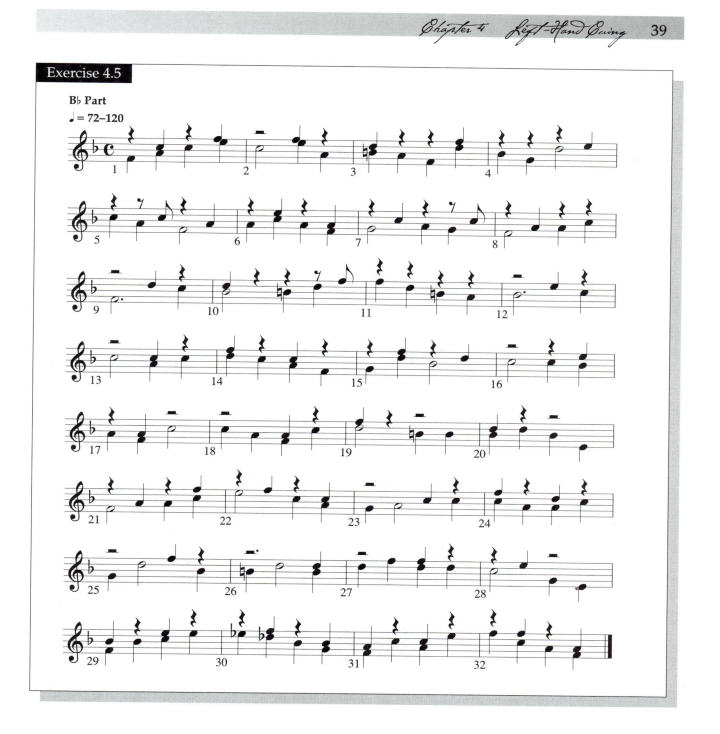

Exercise 4.6

Bass Part

♩ = 72–120

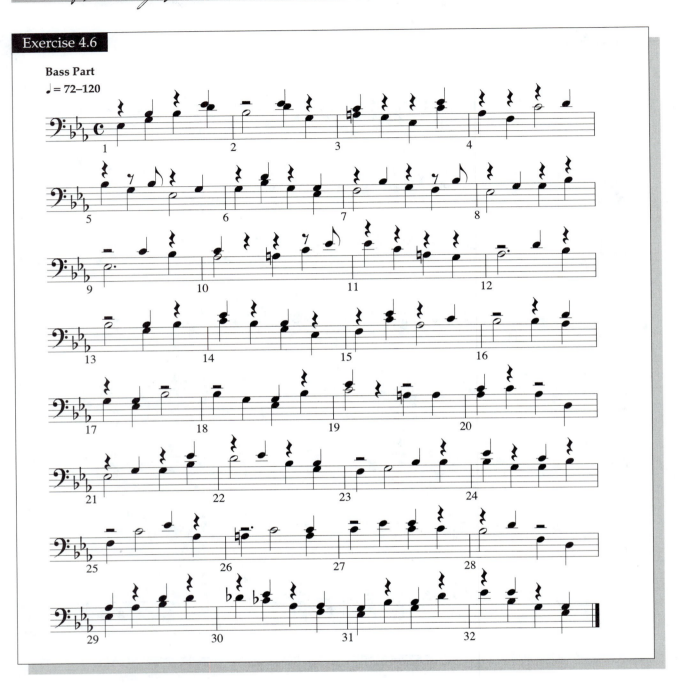

Left-Hand Cuing with Right-Hand Conducting

Exercise 4.6

Objective: Coordinate left-hand cuing with a right-hand conducting pattern.

1. Cue *every eighth note and quarter note* with the left hand.

2. One half of the class plays the lower notes; the other half plays the cued notes *only* if cued (♩ = 72–120).

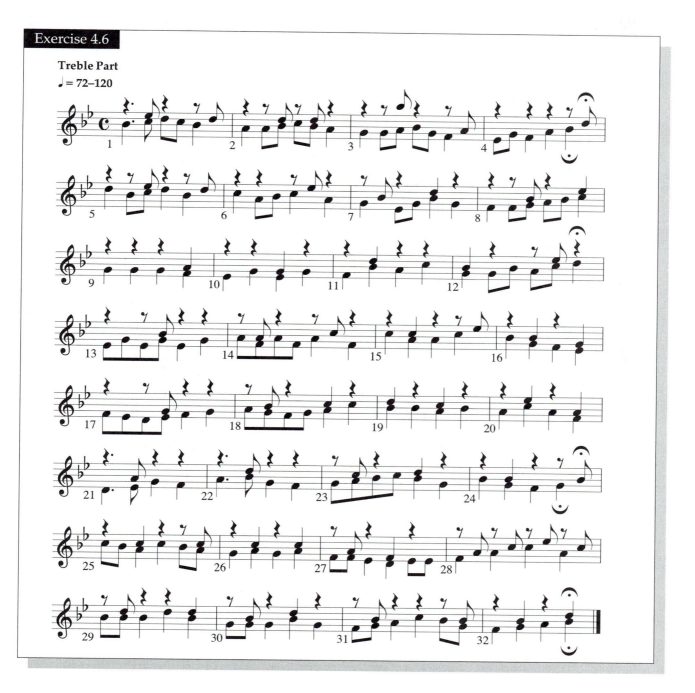

Exercise 4.6

F Part

♩ = 72–120

Exercise 4.6

E♭ Part

♩ = 72–120

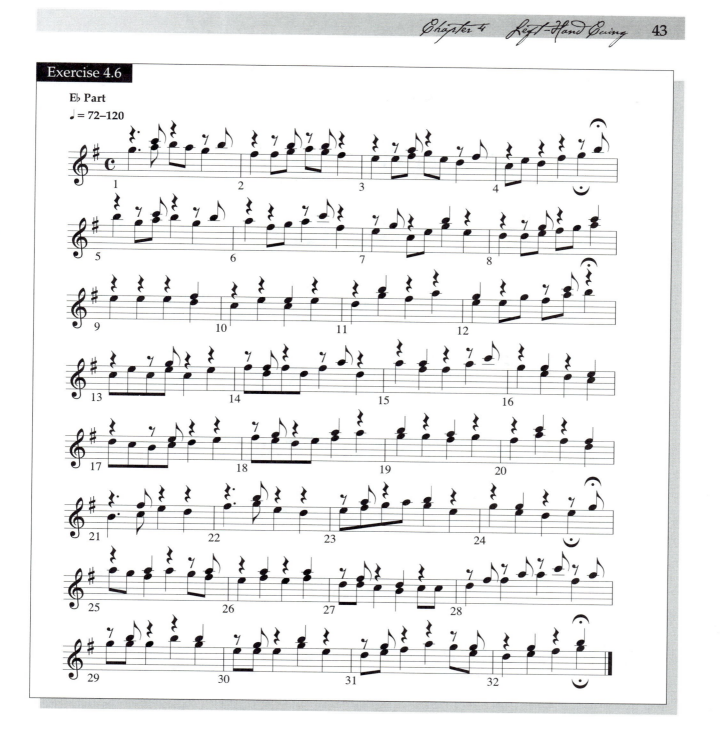

Exercise 4.6

B♭ Part

♩ = 72–120

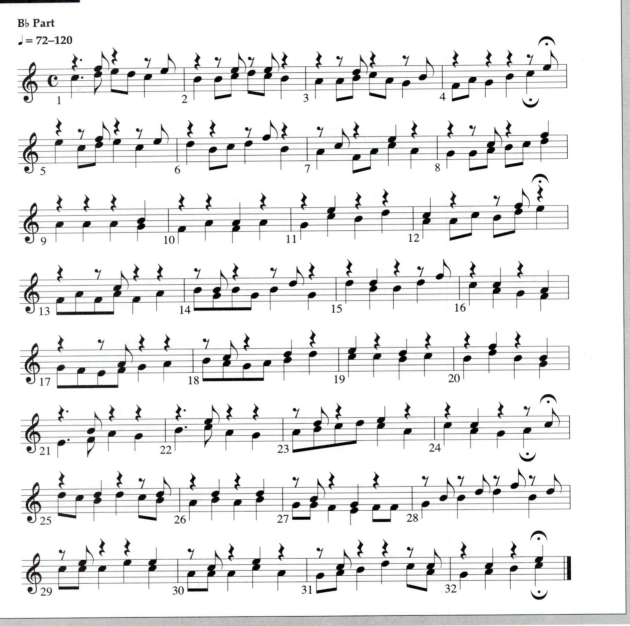

Exercise 4.6

Bass Part

♩ = 72–120

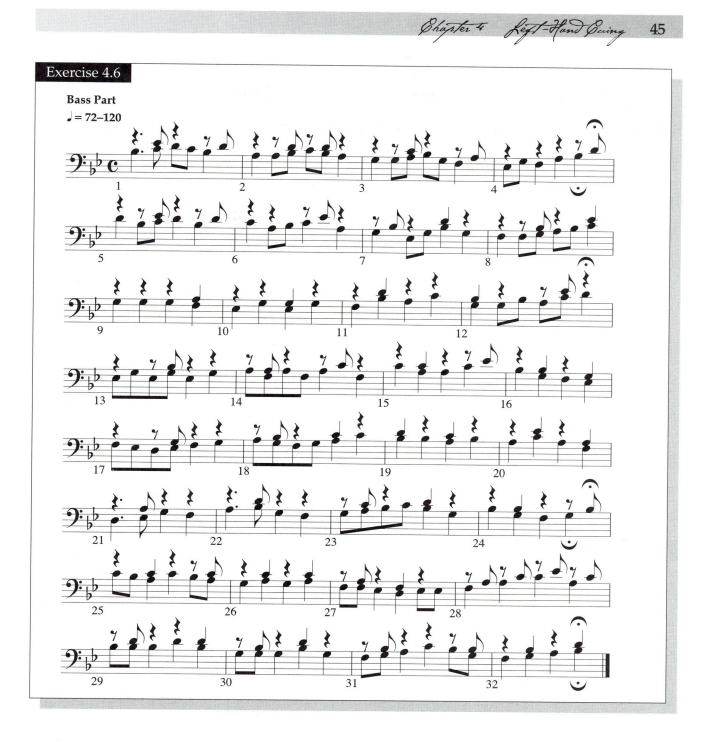

Coordinating Cues with Conducting

Exercise 5.1 *Left-Hand Cuing with Right-Hand Conducting*

Objective: Coordinate left-hand cuing with right-hand conducting patterns, fermati, and releases.

1. Right-hand players play a chosen scale using one scale step per measure.

2. Left-hand players play the scale chosen, starting a third higher.

3. Conduct fermati with and without a caesura. Use correct releases for each hand.

4. Release all left-hand fermati with the left hand, right-hand fermati with the right hand.

5. Some students may find it beneficial to practice each hand separately before using both hands ($\quarternote$ = 96–120).

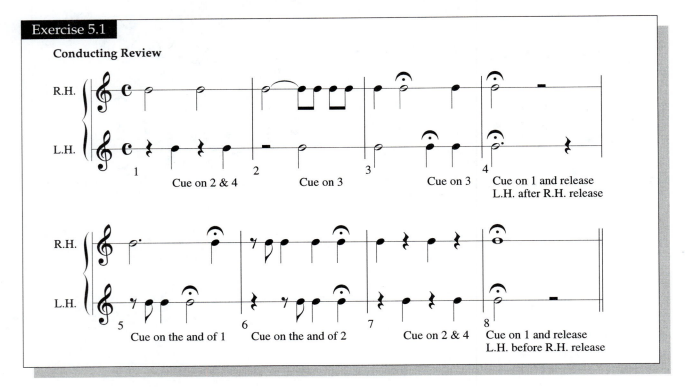

Exercise 5.1

Conducting Review

Left-Hand Cuing with Right-Hand Conducting

Exercise 5.2

Objective: Coordinate left-hand cuing with right-hand conducting patterns, fermati, and releases.

This is a harmonized version of Exercise 5.1. Follow the same instructions, particularly releasing all left-hand fermati with the left hand and right-hand fermati with the right hand.

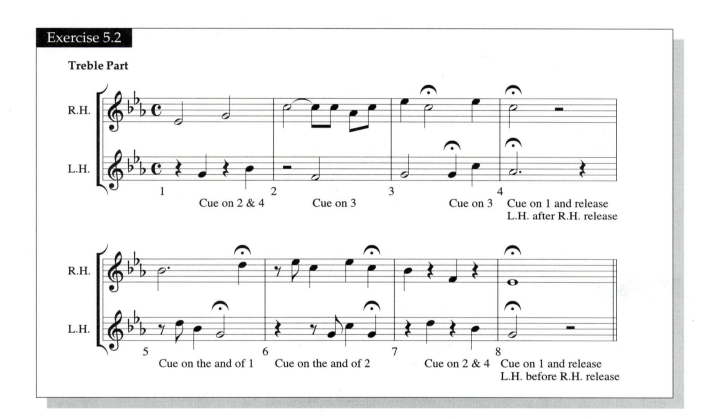

Exercise 5.2

F Part

Exercise 5.2

E♭ Part

Exercise 5.2

Bb Part

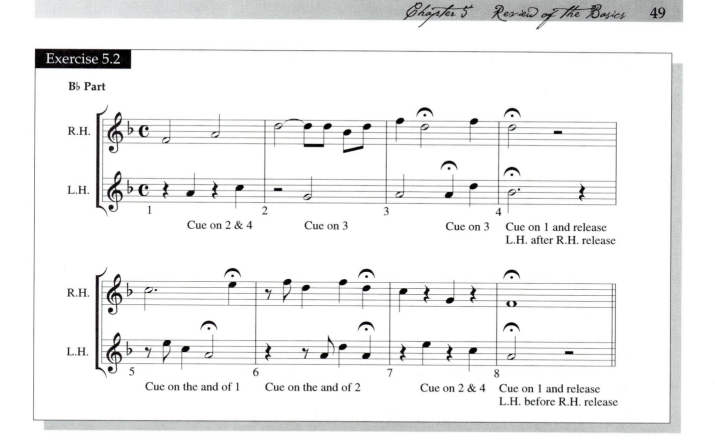

Exercise 5.2

Bass Part

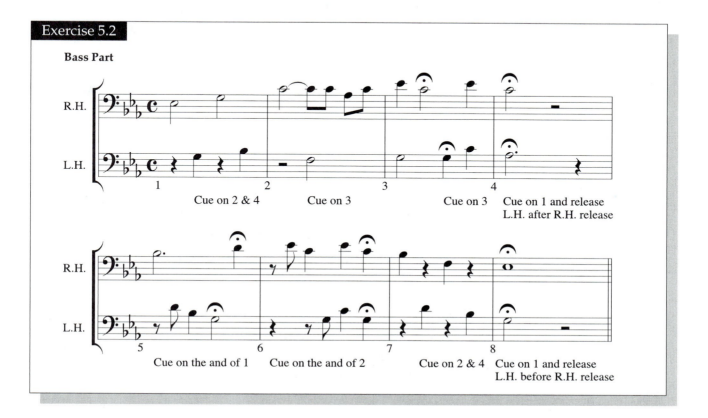

Conducting the Specific Seating Arrangement

Exercise 5.3   Cuing a Specific Musician or Section

Objective: Cue specific instruments in a specific seating arrangement.

Use the seating arrangement below for the conducting exercises that follow. In classes with incomplete instrumentation, any instrument may substitute for any other.

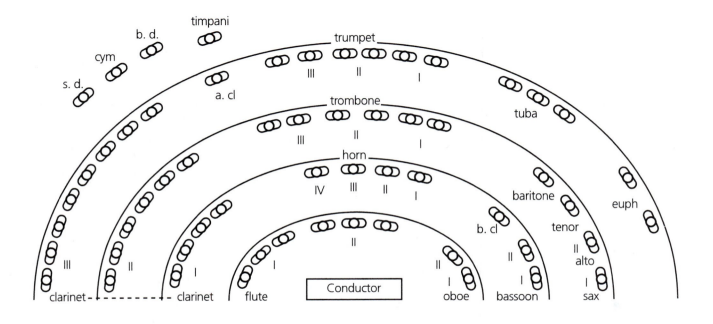

To the conductor:

1. Select any major or minor scale. Play one scale step per measure. Do not repeat top pitch of the scale.

2. Use the seating diagram for exact cuing direction.

3. Conduct in a legato style except for accented notes.

To the players:

4. If conductor does not cue you, do not play your entrance.

5. When you are cued, play *forte* one scale step above the scale step that the ensemble is playing.

Exercise 5.3

Conducting Review

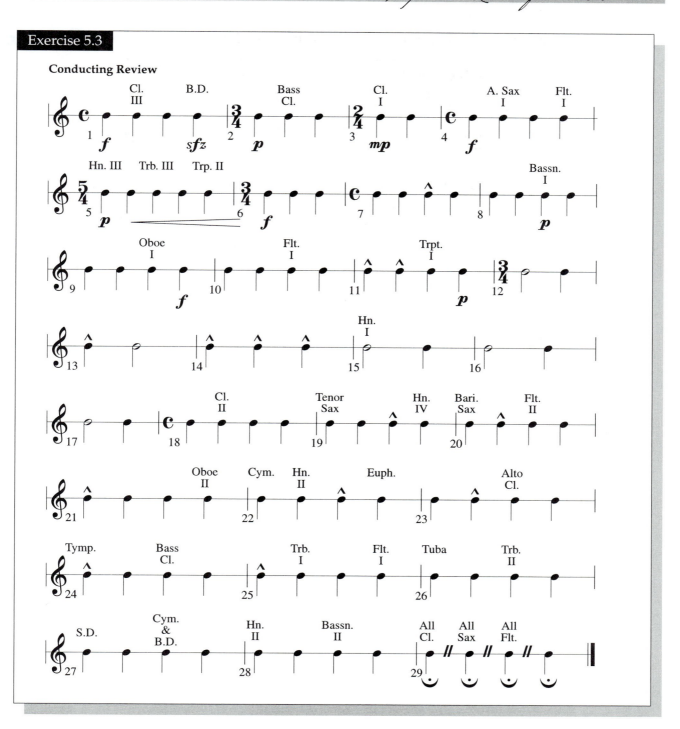

Exercise 5.4   Cuing a Specific Musician or Section

Objective: Cue specific instruments in a specific seating arrangement.

Conduct in a legato style except for accented notes. The players follow these instructions:

1. If the conductor does not cue you, do not play your entrance.

2. When you are cued, play *forte*. Each cued note is played with the note that follows. For example, in measure one, play the Cl. III cue on the second beat with the second quarter note.

Exercise 5.4

Treble Part

Exercise 5.4

F Part

Exercise 5.4

Eb Part

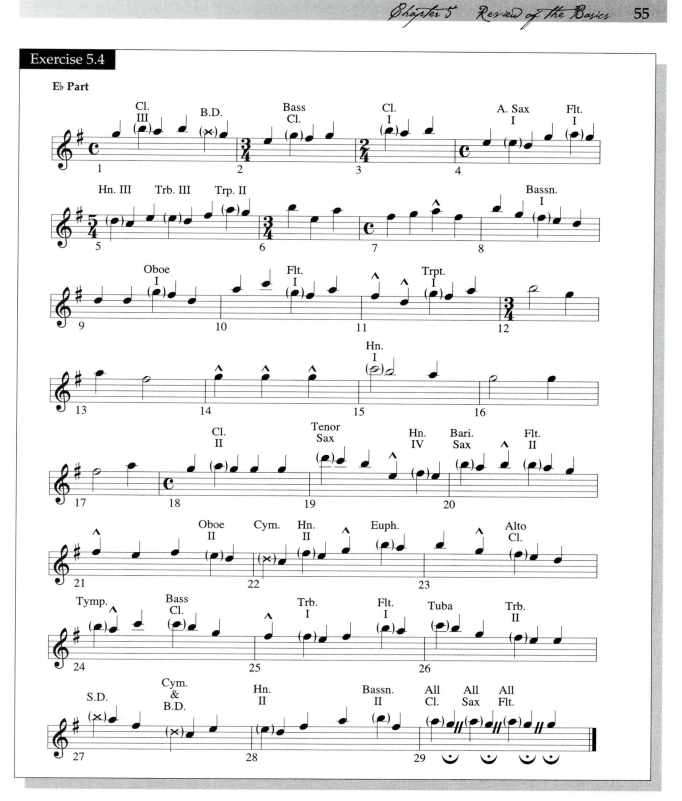

Exercise 5.4

Bb Part

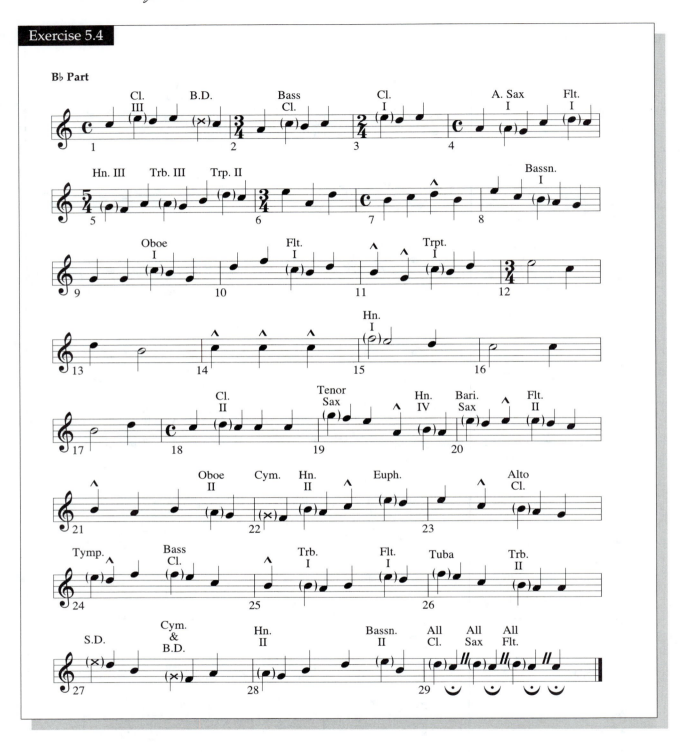

Exercise 5.4

Bass Part

Cuing a Specific Musician or Section   *Exercise 5.5*

Exercise 5.5

Treble Part

Exercise 5.5

F Part

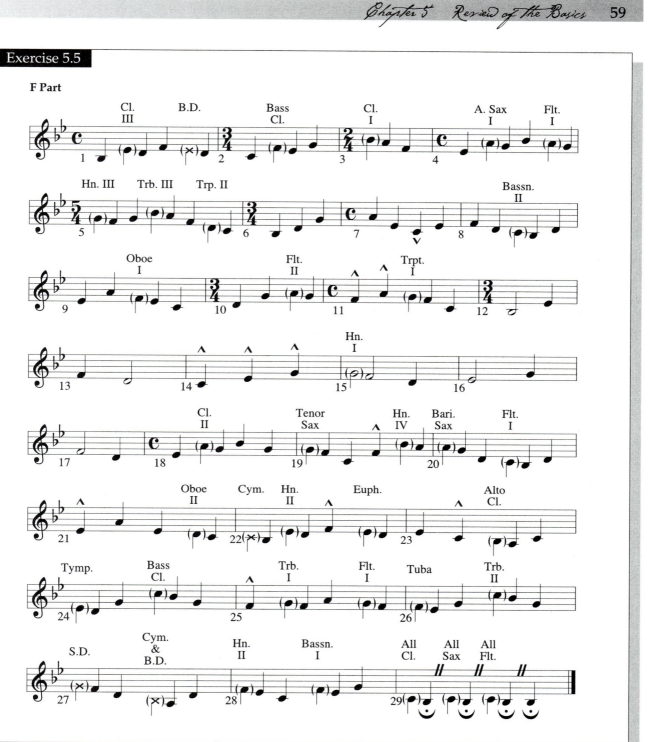

Exercise 5.5

Eb Part

Exercise 5.5

B♭ Part

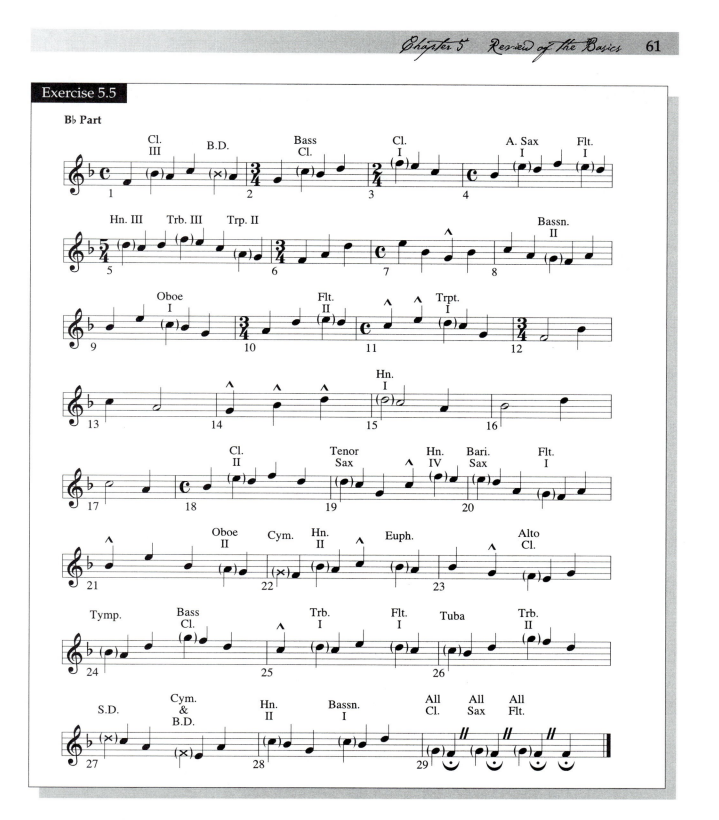

Exercise 5.5

Bass Part

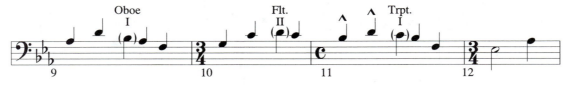

CHAPTER 6

Dynamics

Left-Hand Control of Dynamics

Left-Hand Dynamic Control   *Exercise 6.1*

Objective: Develop control of dynamics using the left hand.

1. For the following exercises, use a metronome set at ♩ = 96–120.
2. Conduct a $\frac{4}{4}$ pattern. With fingers of the left hand pointing toward the floor and left palm facing forward, fully extend your left arm and hand above your head, rotating your wrist and using a full range of motion. At the top of the extension, turn your palm forward and return to the original position with fingers pointing toward the floor and palm facing forward.
3. Conduct a $\frac{3}{4}$ pattern and repeat the left-hand exercise.
4. Conduct a $\frac{2}{4}$ pattern and repeat the left-hand exercise.
5. Conduct a $\frac{6}{8}$ pattern and repeat the left-hand exercise.

Left-Hand Dynamic Control   *Exercise 6.2*

1. Play the following examples in the appropriate octave and range for your instrument. Switch octaves if necessary.
2. First, conduct one line. Next time on the podium, conduct four lines of an example with no stop.

Exercise 6.2

Treble Part

♩ = 96–120

Exercise 6.2

Treble Part *(continued)*

Exercise 6.2

Treble Part (*continued*)

Exercise 6.2

Treble Part (continued)

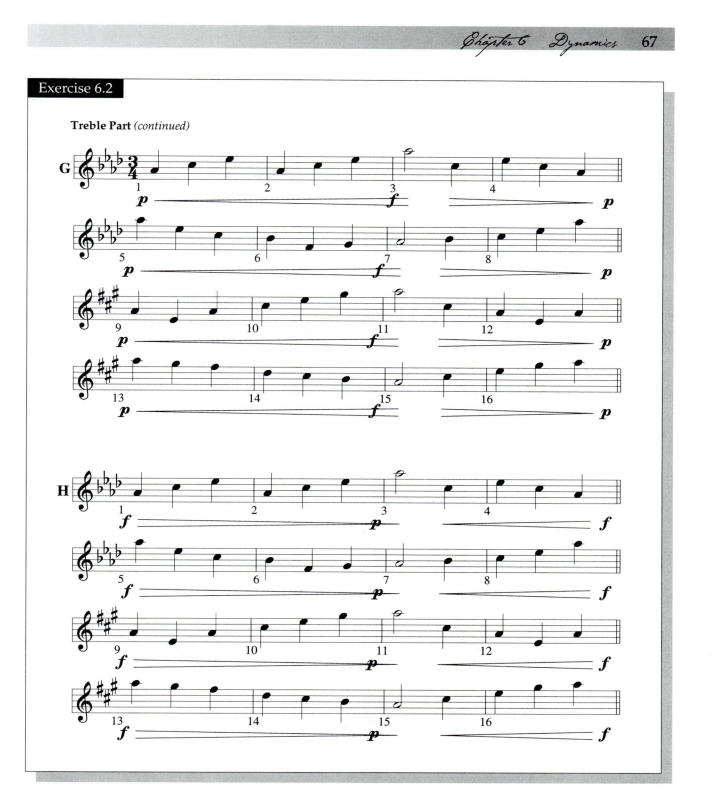

Exercise 6.2

F Part

♩ = 96–120

Exercise 6.2

F Part (continued)

Exercise 6.2

F Part (continued)

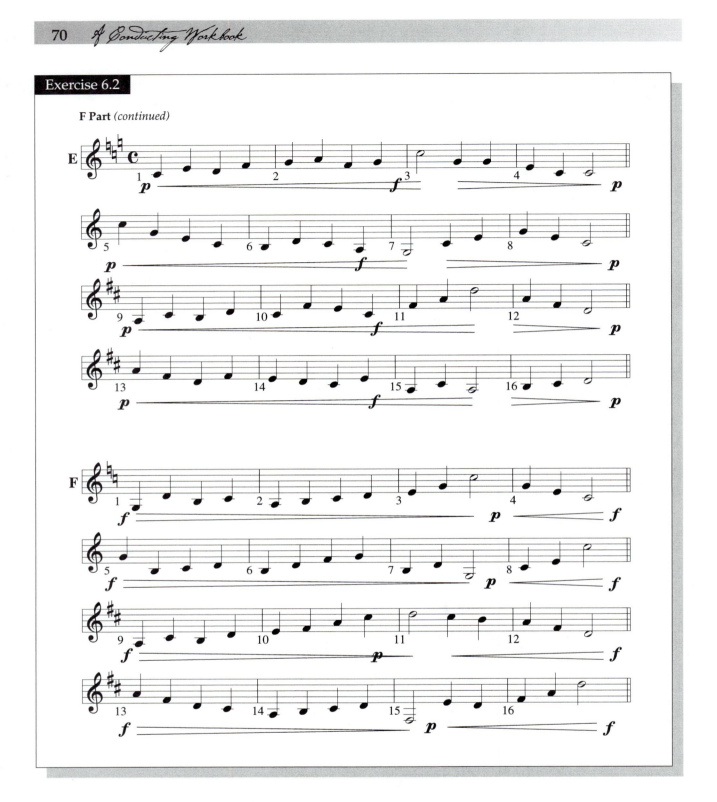

Exercise 6.2

F Part (continued)

Exercise 6.2

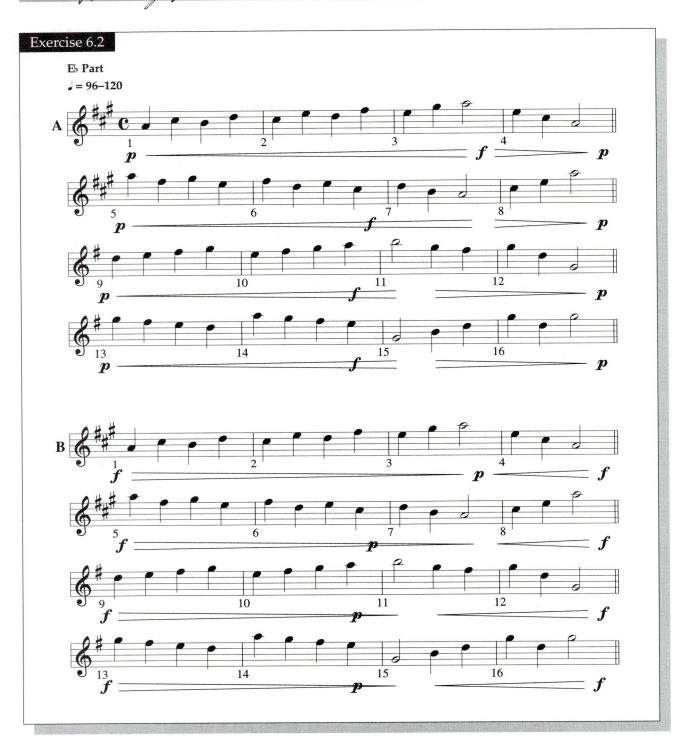

Exercise 6.2

E♭ Part (*continued*)

Exercise 6.2

E♭ Part (*continued*)

Exercise 6.2

E♭ Part (*continued*)

Exercise 6.2

B♭ Part

♩ = 96–120

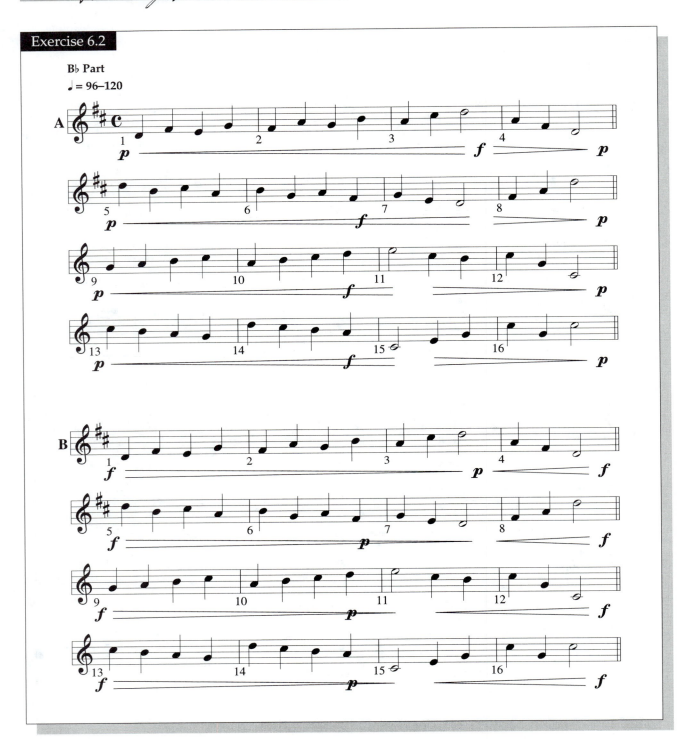

Exercise 6.2

B♭ Part (continued)

Exercise 6.2

Bb Part (*continued*)

Exercise 6.2

B♭ Part (continued)

Exercise 6.2

Bass Part

♩ = 96–120

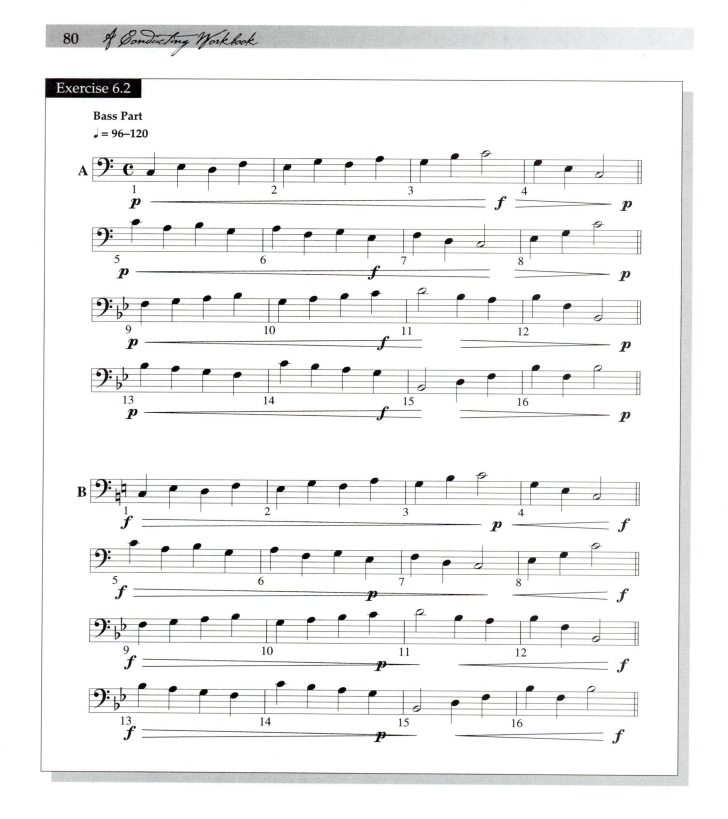

Exercise 6.2

Bass Part (*continued*)

Exercise 6.2

Bass Part (*continued*)

Exercise 6.2

Bass Part (*continued*)

CHAPTER 7

Mixed Meter

ith so much music written using mixed meter, the conductor must not only know how to conduct mixed meter but also how to rehearse and explain the way mixed meter functions.

Breaking Down the Meter

Generally, breaking the pulse down to its smallest denominator will provide rhythmic stability for the players and allow the conductor to give the players a beat pattern that is accurate and easily readable. For example, you would conduct a $\frac{5}{8}$ measure of 2 + 3 eighth notes by using a two-pattern that gives the second half of the pattern three eighth notes of time. A $\frac{5}{8}$ measure divided 3 + 2 would use a two-pattern that places the three eighth notes into the first half of the pattern. You would use the loop two-pattern, not the fishhook.

Use a standard three-pattern to conduct a $\frac{7}{8}$ measure. Determine where in the three-pattern you would accommodate the three eighth notes of time by looking at how the measure is constructed rhythmically. For example, conduct a 2 + 2 + 3 meter by using a three-pattern with the three eighth notes in the third stroke of the pattern. Conduct 2 + 3 + 2 by using a three-pattern with the three eighth notes in the second stroke of the pattern. Then conduct 3 + 2 + 2 by using a three-pattern with the three eighth notes in the first stroke of the pattern.

Allow enough time and duration to accommodate the part of the beat pattern that demands the extra pulse.

Exercise 7.1   Mixed Meter with Metronome

Objective: Prepare for conducting mixed meter.

---

1. Use neither music nor ensemble.

2. Set metronome at $\flat$ = 160.

3. Begin with a given configuration of mixed meter (possibly from your instructor) and conduct a variety of time signatures using basic beat patterns: $\frac{2}{4}$ for $\frac{5}{8}$, $\frac{3}{4}$ for $\frac{7}{8}$, and so on.

Mixed Meter with Scales   *Exercise 7.2*

Objective: Conduct changing time signatures while keeping a
steady pulse ($\flat$ = 160).

1. Conductors can practice alone with a metronome or with a class ensem-
    ble. Use these basic patterns to conduct the mixed meter examples:

    ■ Regular loop two-pattern for $\frac{5}{8}$

    ■ Regular three-pattern for $\frac{7}{8}$

    ■ Regular three-pattern for $\frac{8}{8}$

    ■ Regular four-pattern for $\frac{11}{8}$

    ■ Regular five-pattern for $\frac{13}{8}$

2. The accompanying diagram shows how to alter a basic pattern to
    accommodate a $\frac{5}{8}$ meter. The same principle applies to all the regular
    patterns.

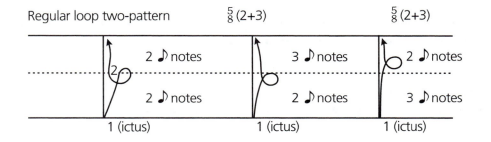

Regular loop two-pattern $\frac{5}{8}$ (2+3) $\frac{5}{8}$ (2+3)

	2 ♪ notes		3 ♪ notes		2 ♪ notes
	2 ♪ notes		2 ♪ notes		3 ♪ notes
1 (ictus)		1 (ictus)		1 (ictus)	

3. Select a scale, then play one scale step for each measure. To end the
    exercise on the tonic, start on the fifth of the chosen scale.

4. Conduct with and without accents—without accents first. When you
    conduct with an accent, give the ictus (where the accent occurs) more
    weight and force than normal.

Exercise 7.2

Practice using different tempi

♪ = 160

Practice with Various Mixed Meters

Mixed Meter in $\frac{5}{8}$ Time

Exercise 7.3

Exercise 7.3

$\frac{5}{8}$ **Treble Part**

♪ = 160

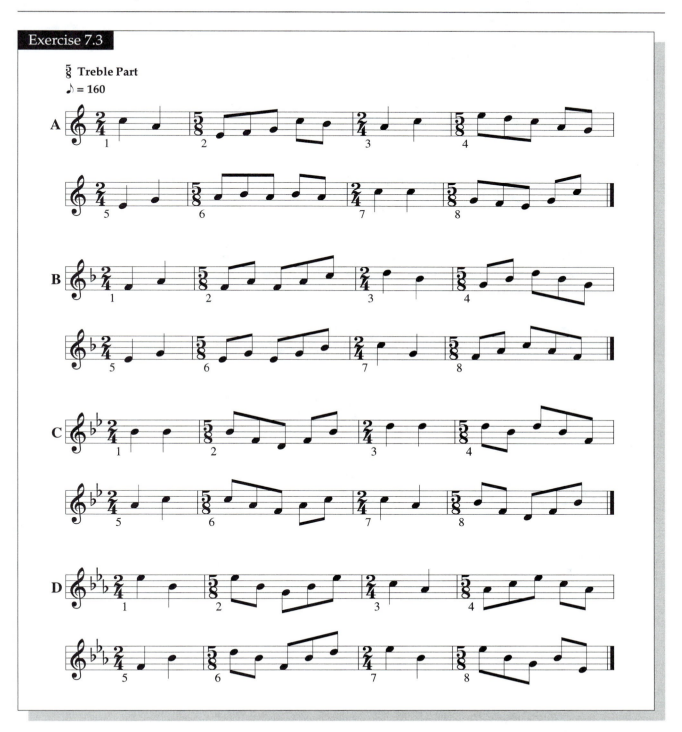

Exercise 7.3

⅝ F Part

♪ = 160

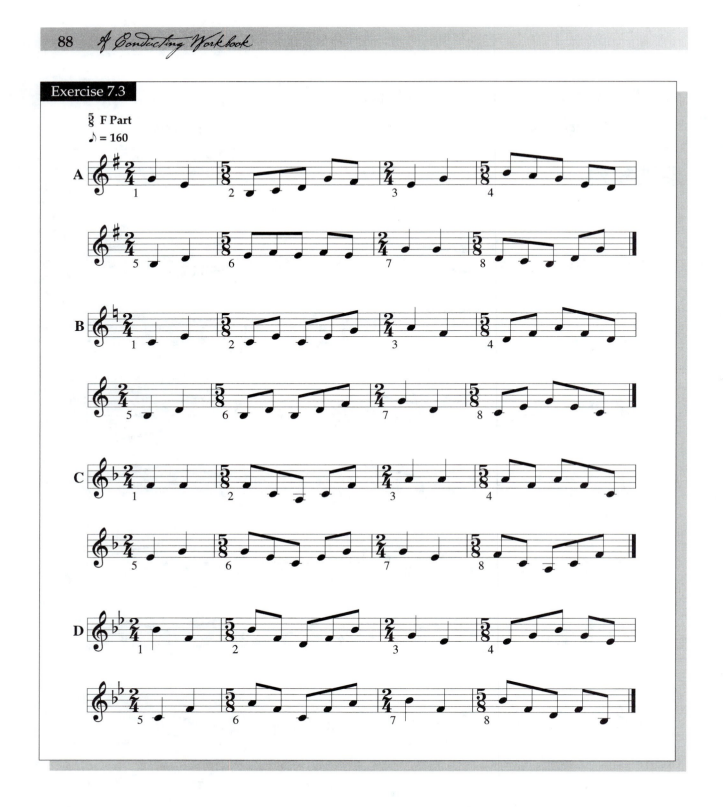

Exercise 7.3

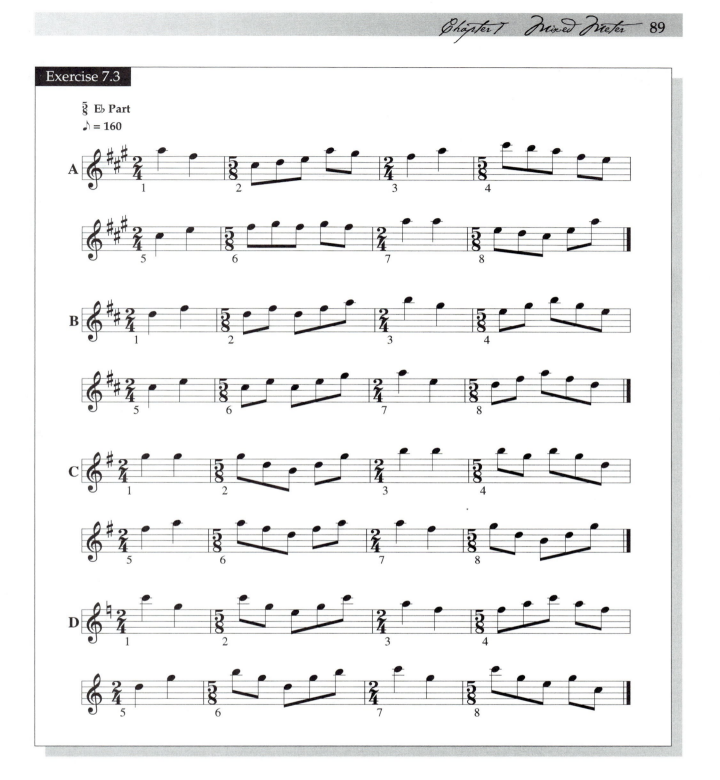

Exercise 7.3

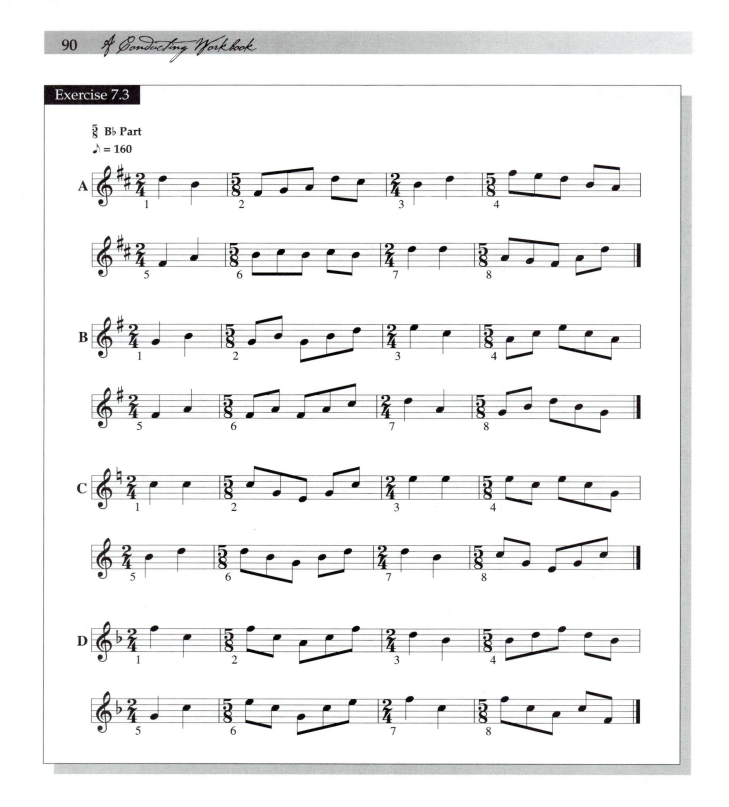

Exercise 7.3

$\frac{5}{8}$ **Bass Part**

♪ = 160

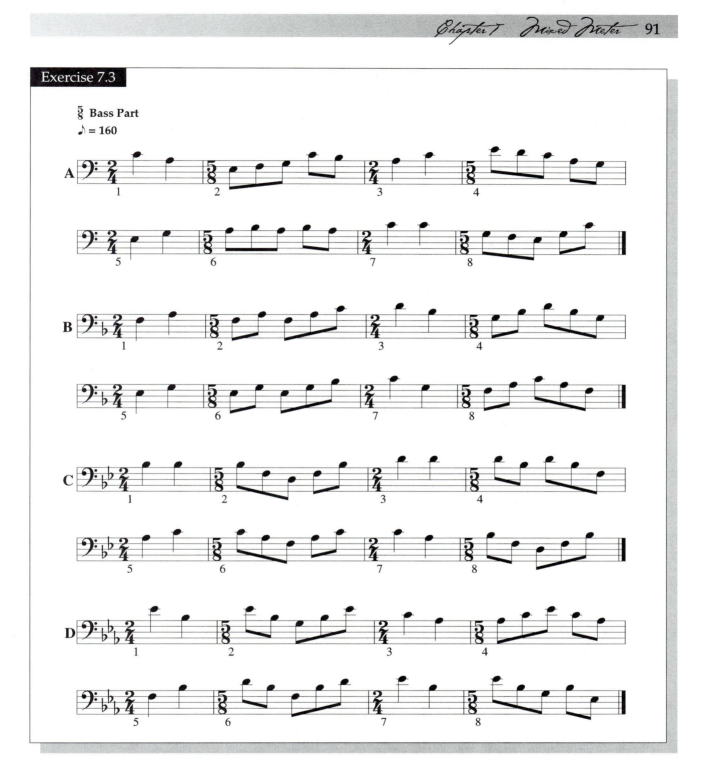

Exercise 7.4   Mixed Meter in ⁷₈ Time

Exercise 7.4

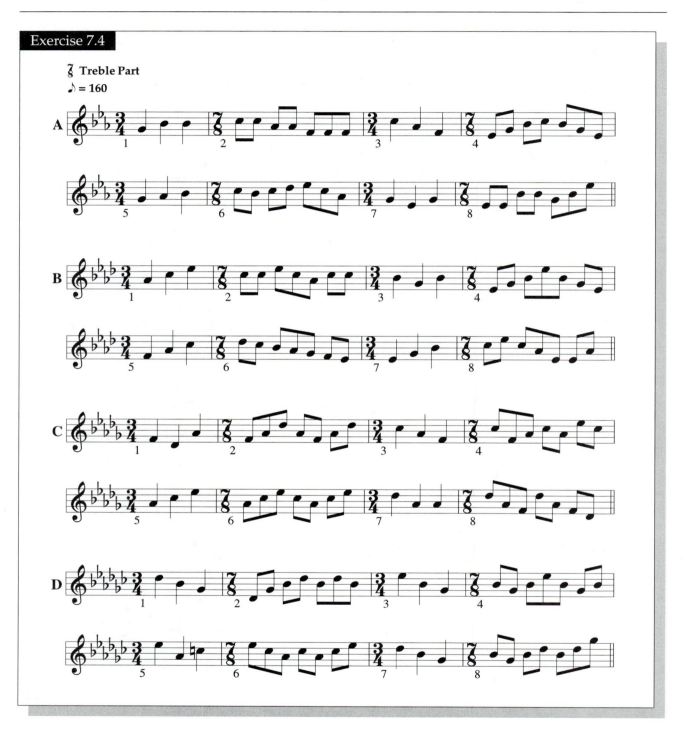

Exercise 7.4

𝄎 F Part

♪ = 160

Exercise 7.4

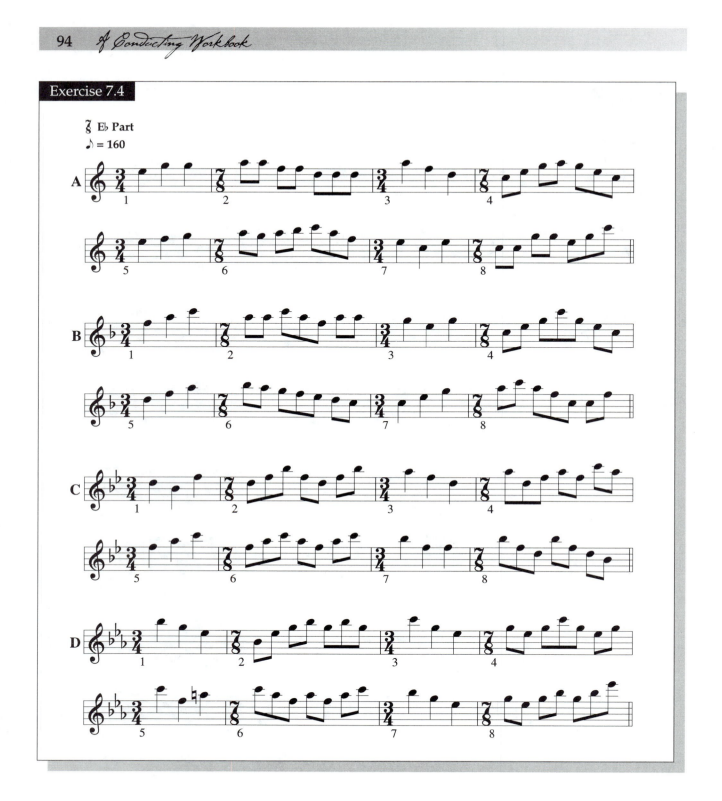

Exercise 7.4

Bb Part

♪ = 160

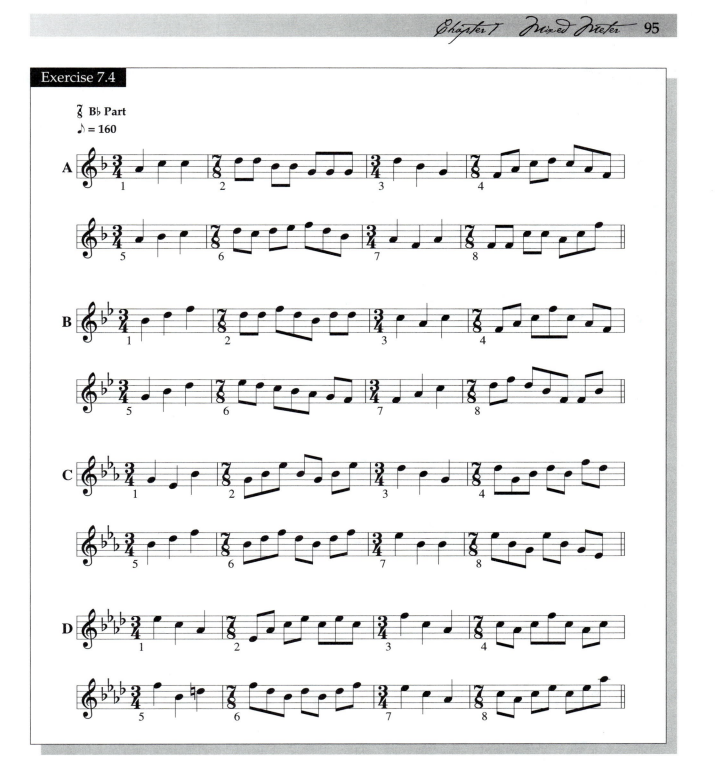

Exercise 7.4

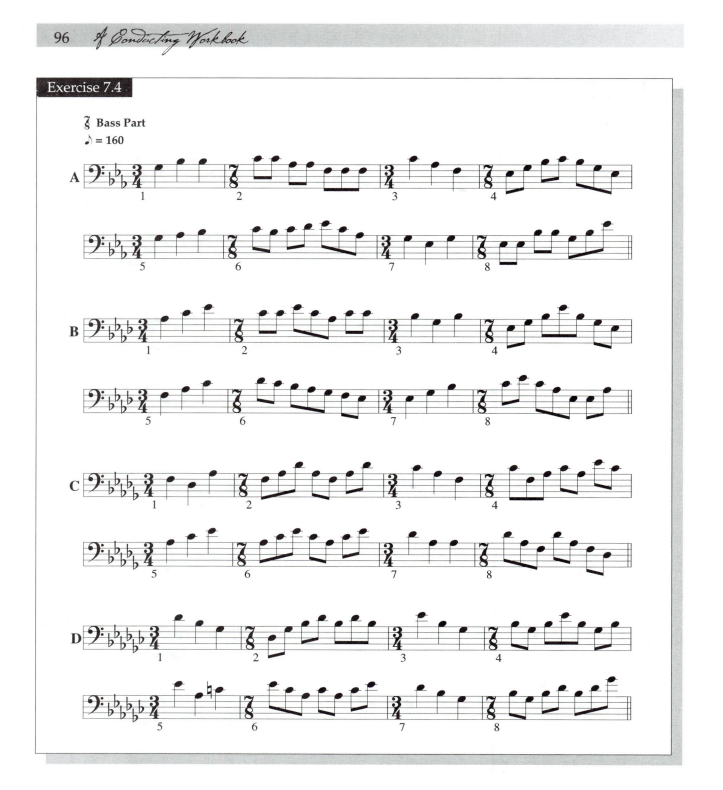

Mixed Meter in ⅜ Time

Exercise 7.5

§ **Treble Part**

♪ = 160

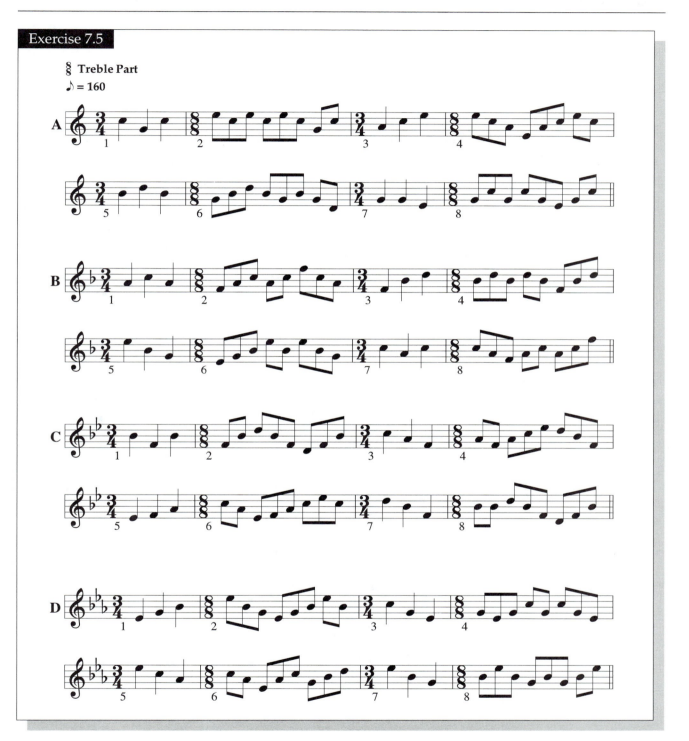

Exercise 7.5

Exercise 7.5

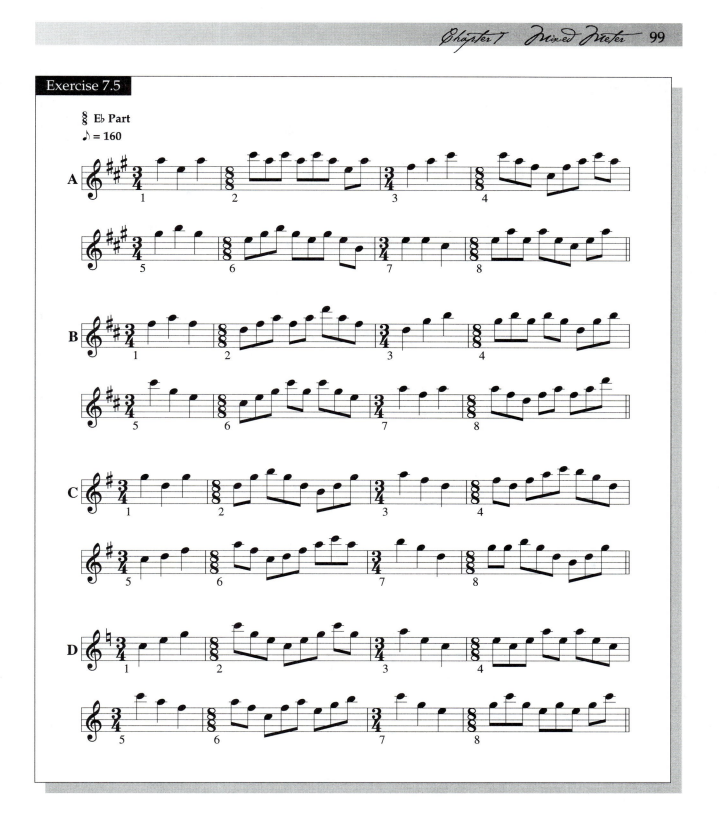

Exercise 7.5

§ B♭ Part

♪ = 160

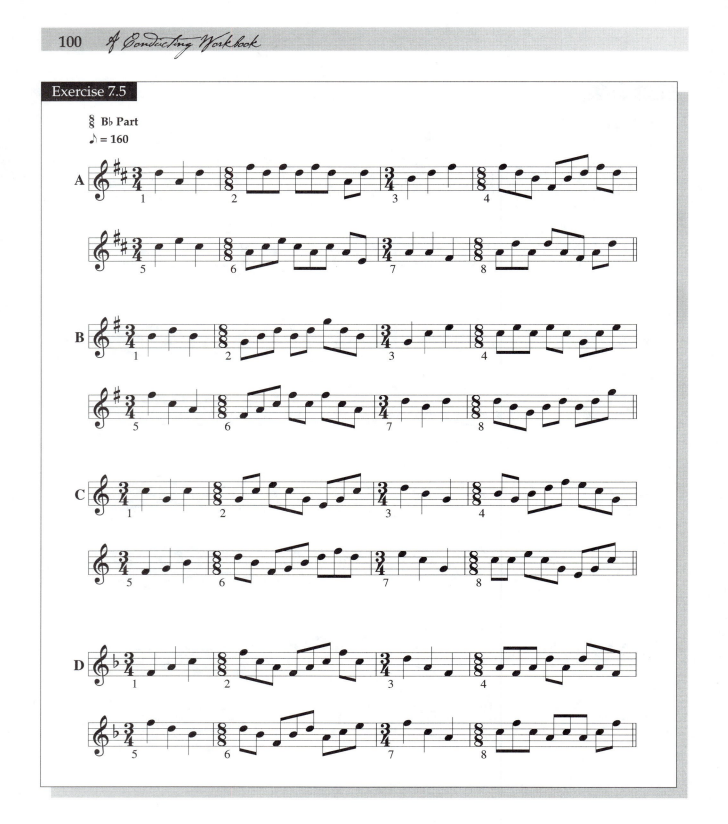

Exercise 7.5

$\frac{8}{8}$ **Bass Part**

♪ = 160

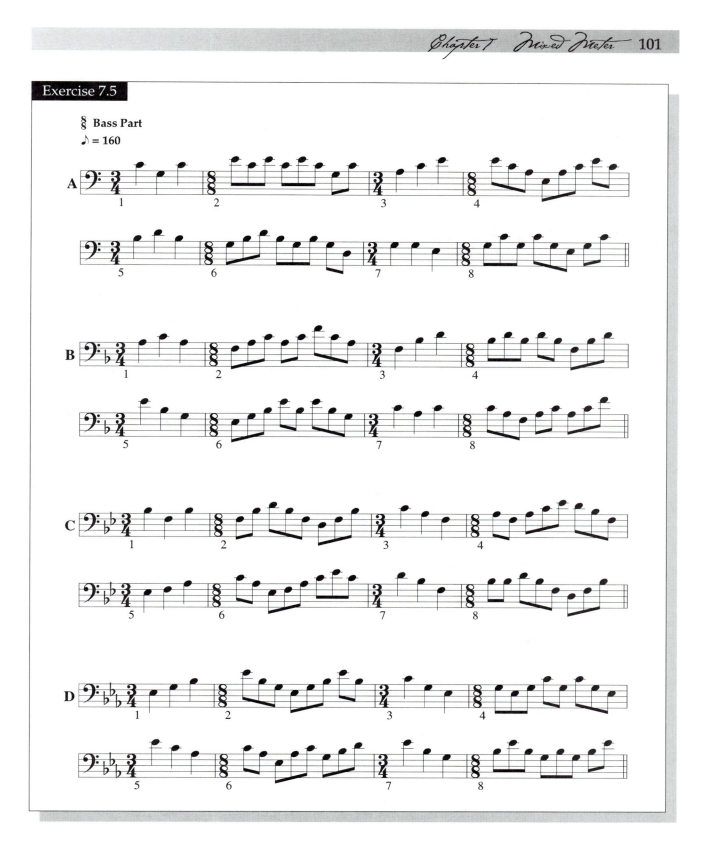

Exercise 7.6   Mixed Meter in $\frac{11}{8}$ Time

Exercise 7.6

Exercise 7.6

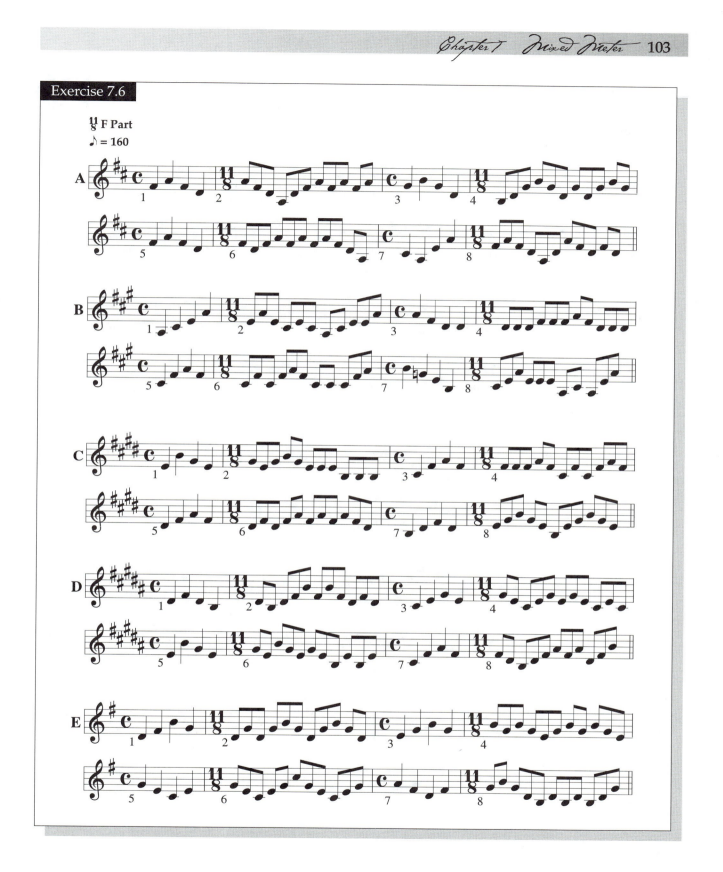

Exercise 7.6

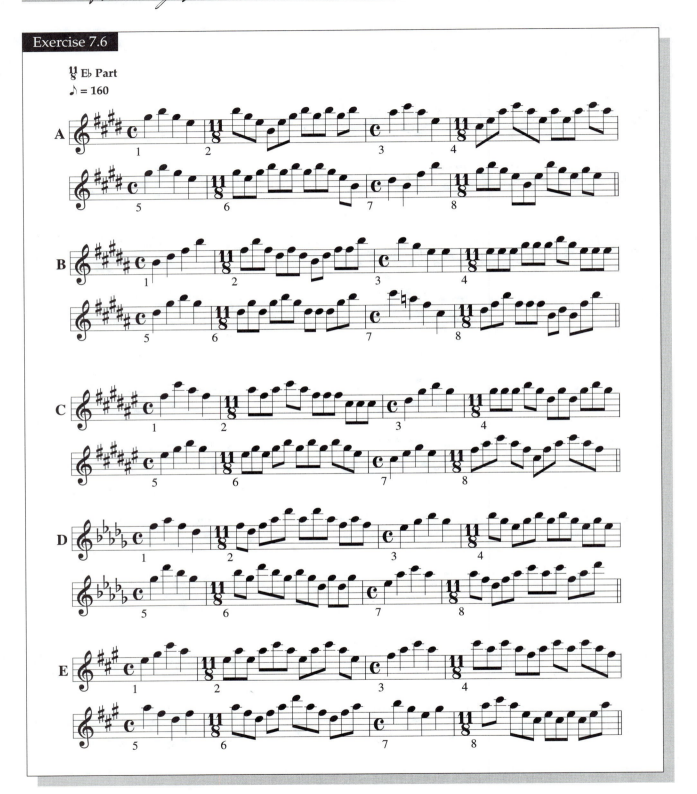

Exercise 7.6

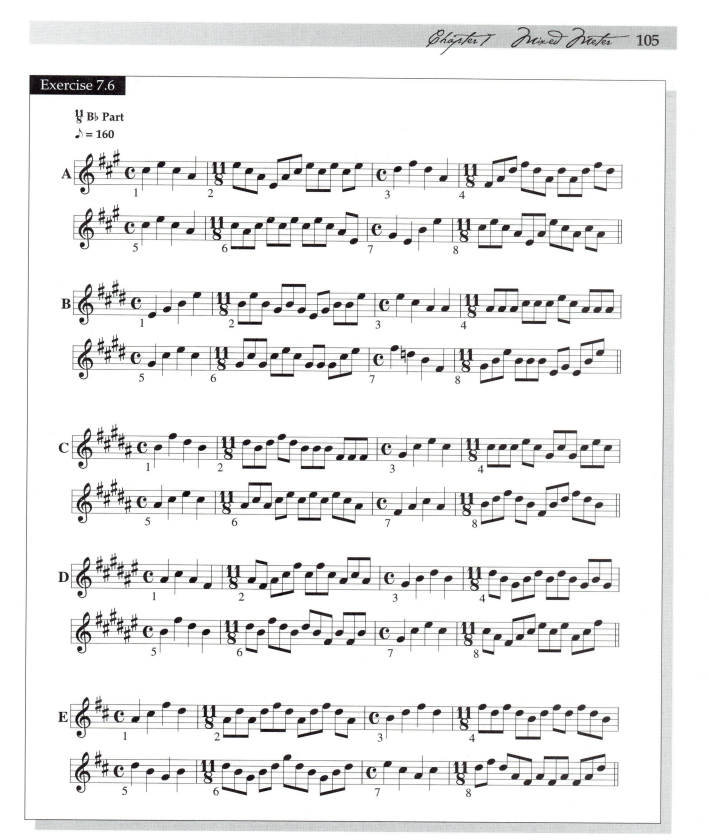

Exercise 7.6

Bass Part

♩ = 160

A

B

C
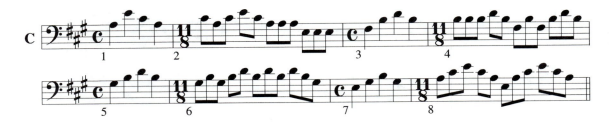

D

E

Mixed Meter in $\frac{13}{8}$ Time   *Exercise 7.7*

$\frac{13}{8}$ **Treble Part**

♪ = 160

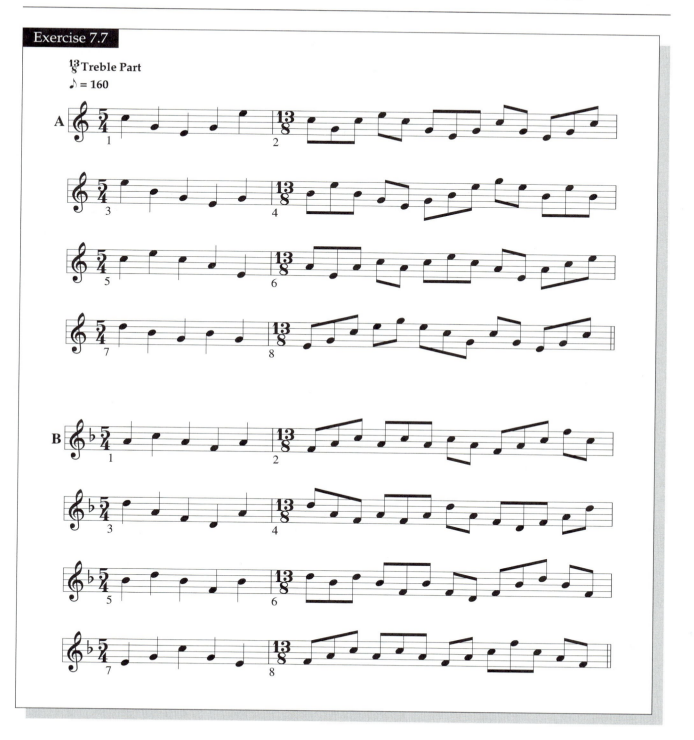

Exercise 7.7

¹³⁄₈ Treble Part (*continued*)

Exercise 7.7

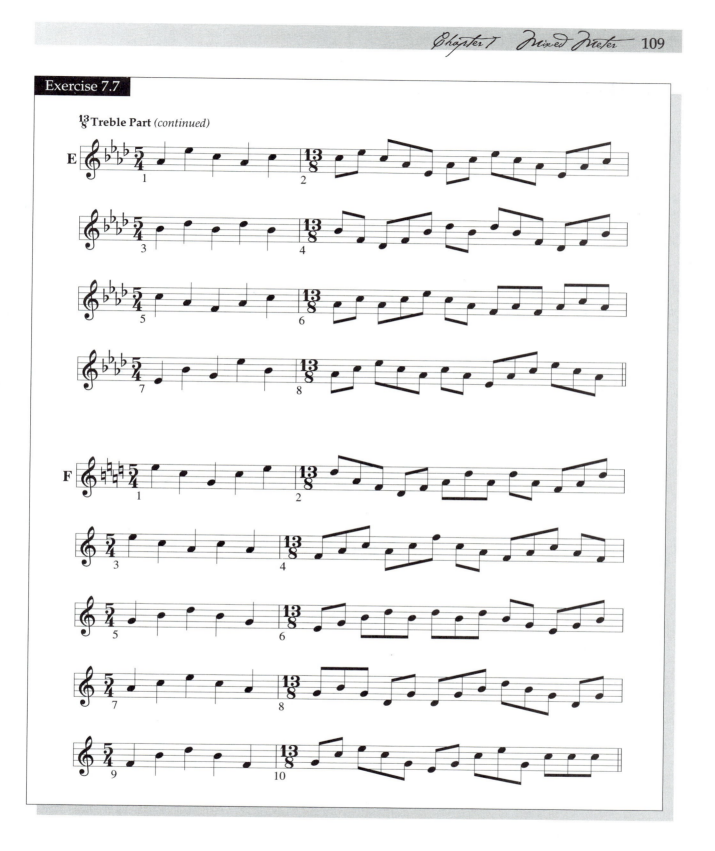

Exercise 7.7

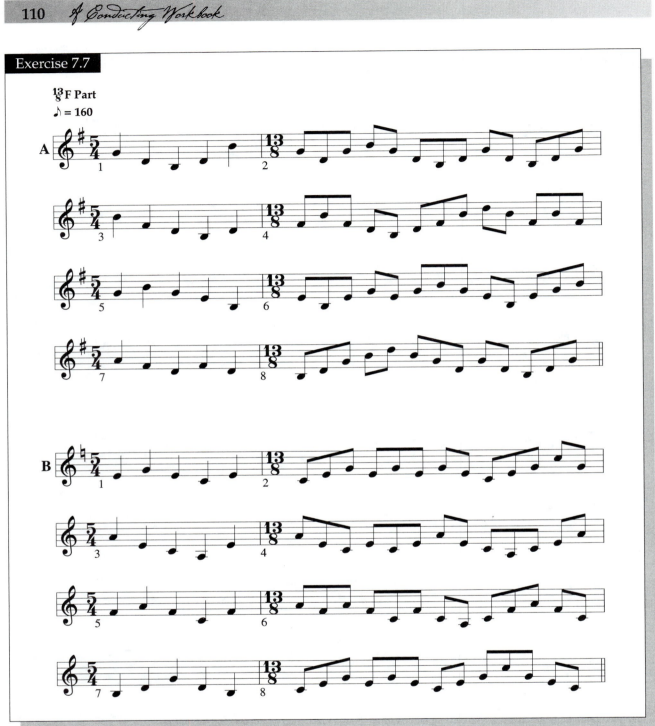

Exercise 7.7

$\frac{13}{8}$ **F Part** *(continued)*

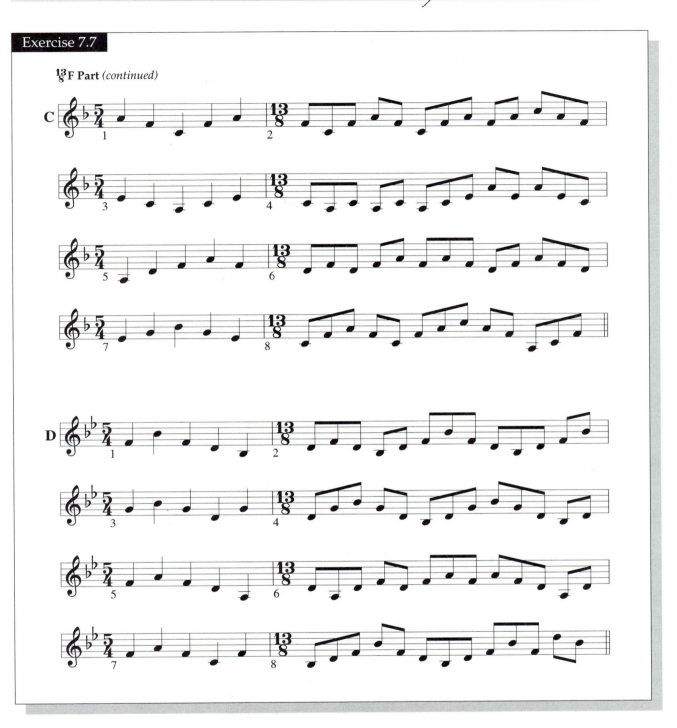

Exercise 7.7

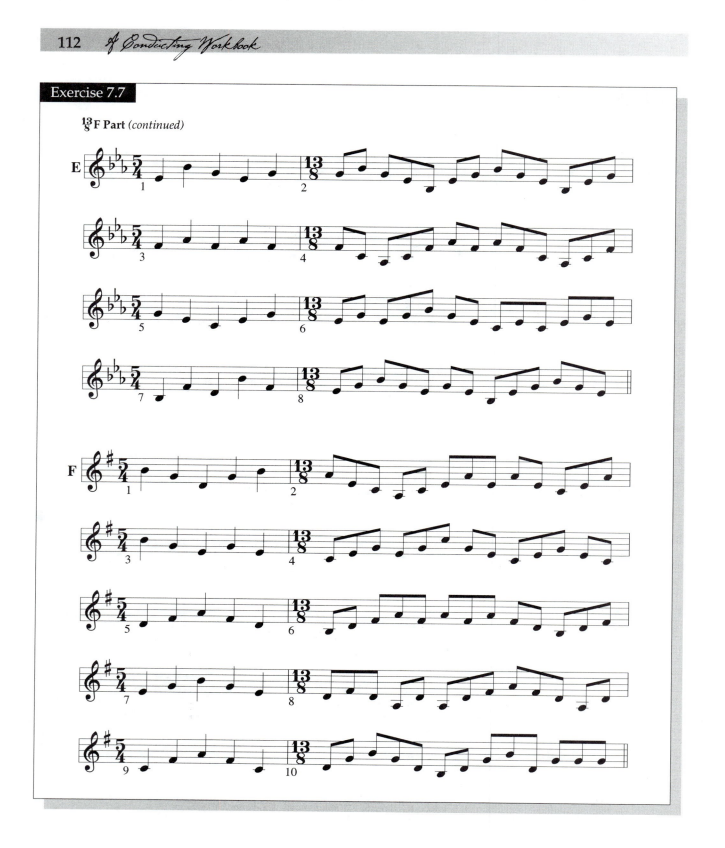

Exercise 7.7

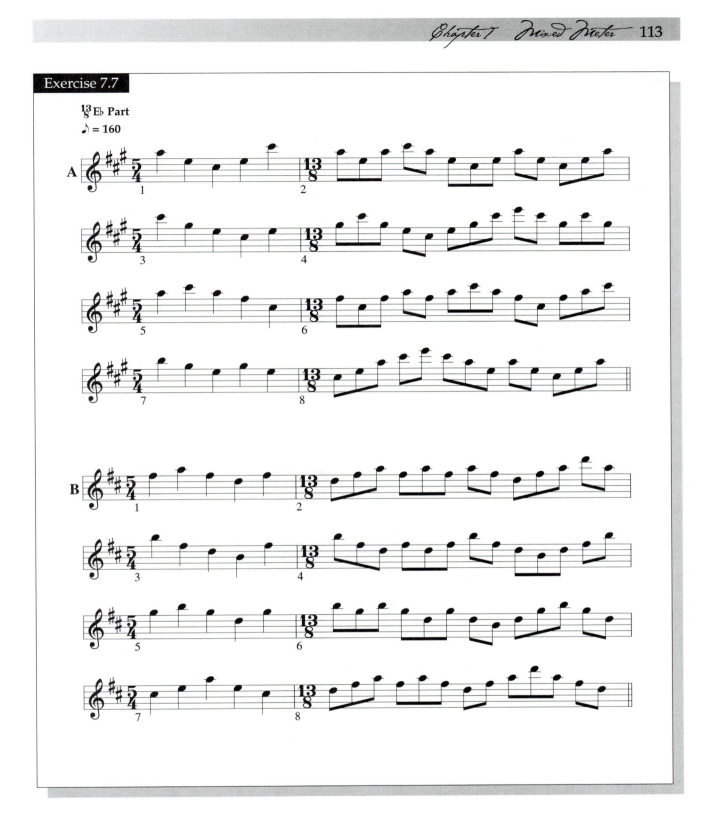

Exercise 7.7

$\frac{13}{8}$ E♭ **Part** (continued)

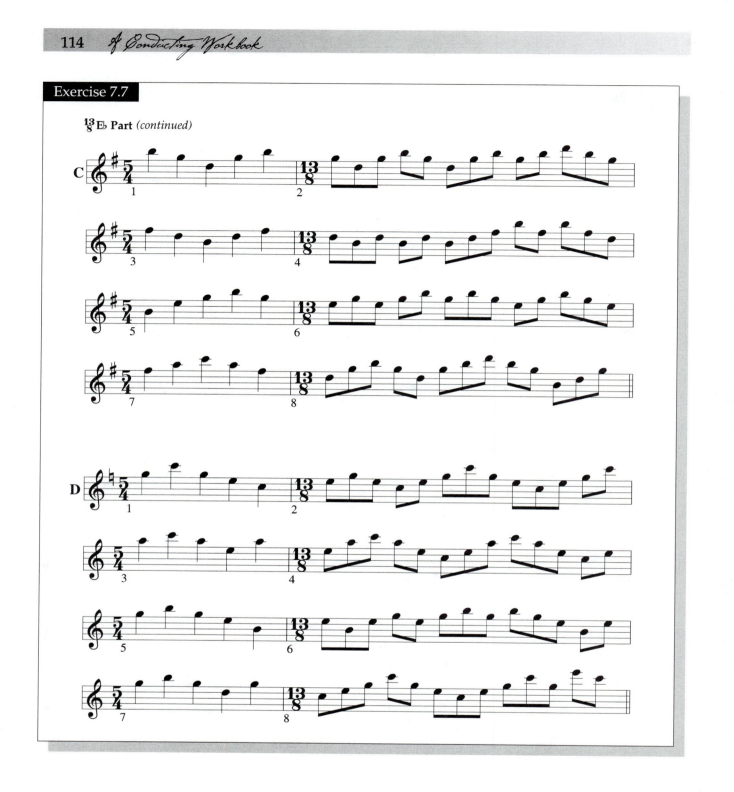

Exercise 7.7

$\frac{13}{8}$ **Eb Part** (*continued*)

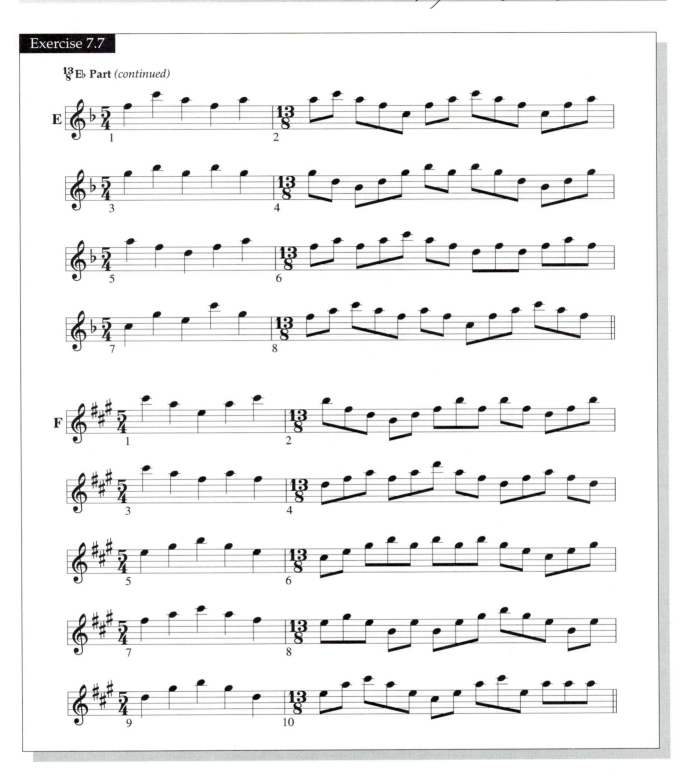

Exercise 7.7

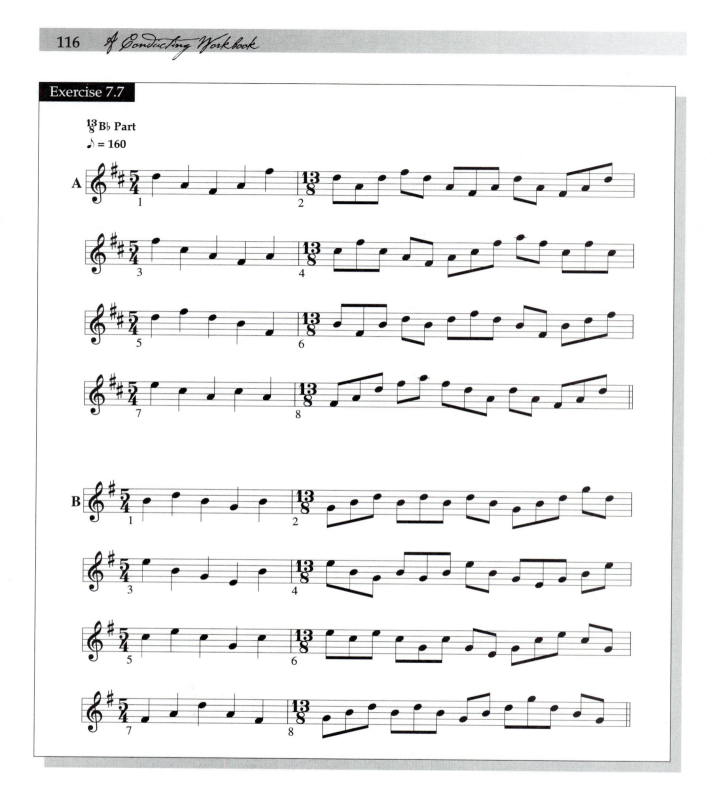

Exercise 7.7

$\frac{13}{8}$ **B♭ Part** (*continued*)

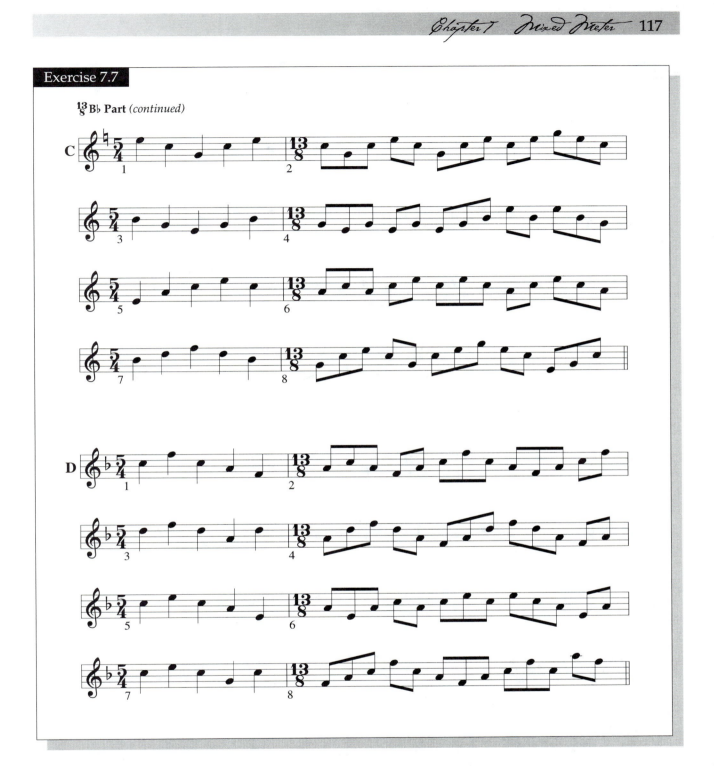

Exercise 7.7

¹³/₈ Bb Part (continued)

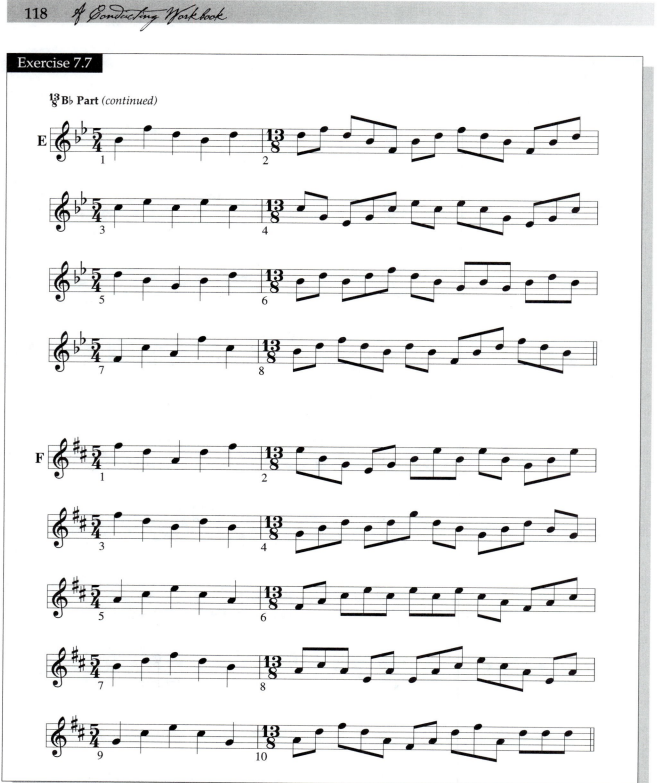

Exercise 7.7

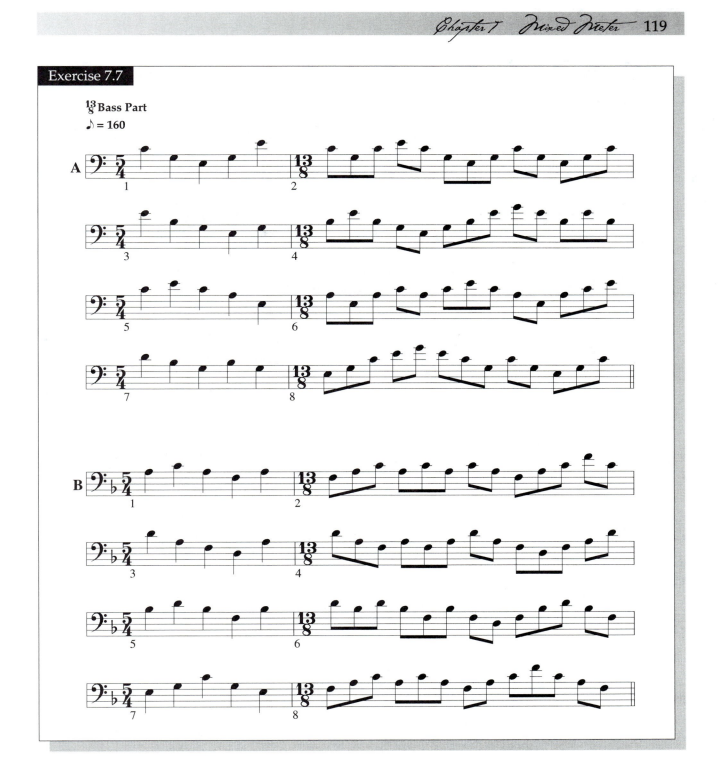

Exercise 7.7

$\frac{13}{8}$ Bass Part (*continued*)

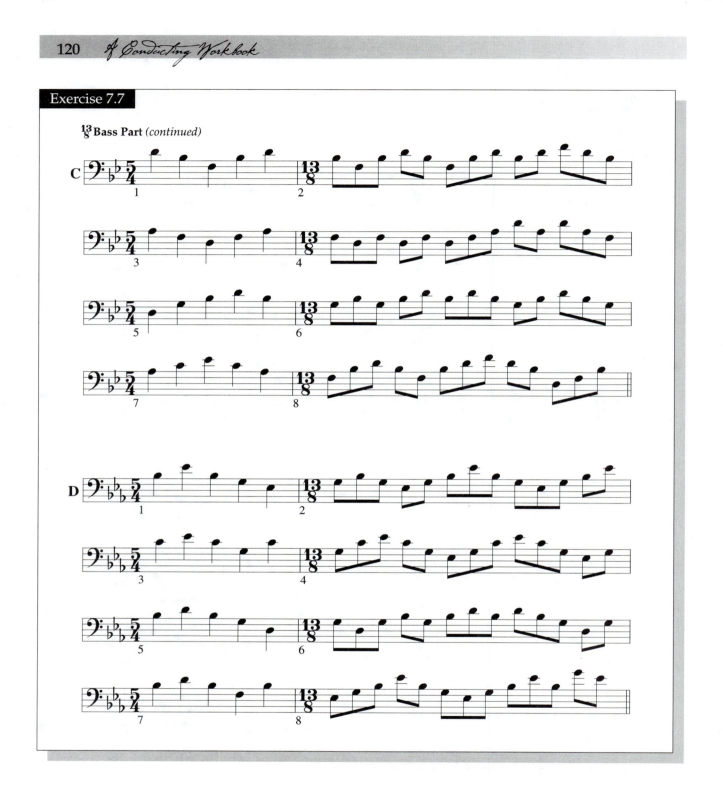

Exercise 7.7

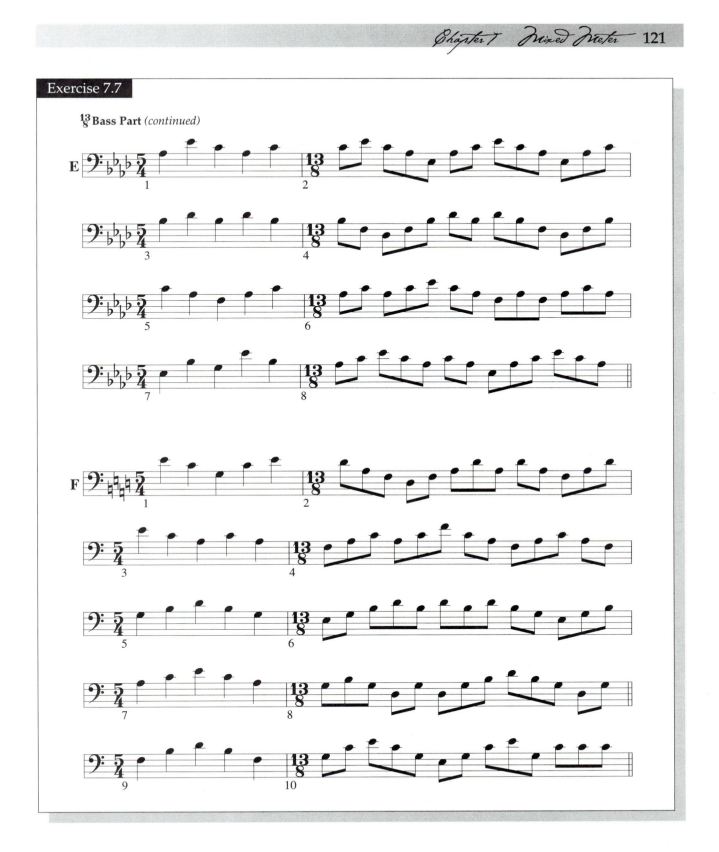

CHAPTER 8   *Conducting Review Exercises*

Mixed Meter Review

The grid presented in this chapter has been generated as a review to further stabilize the mechanics and musicality of conducting mixed meter. Using the grid as instructed will enhance your muscle memory as you conduct an ensemble. You will need to be very secure in your conducting patterns of mixed meter unless you have an ensemble that is mature enough and musically advanced enough to bring their own experience to what you are conducting from the podium.

An additional purpose of practicing with the grid is to make the following exercises easier to conduct, which in turn should enable the players to read and follow your conducting patterns with no confusion.

Exercise 8.1   *Mixed Meter*

1. Set metronome at ♪ = 160.

2. Use the mixed meter grid that follows.

3. First, conduct sequentially line A, B, C, and so on.

4. Then, mix cells as technique allows—for example, A1, B2, C3, D4, D5, and so on.

Mixed Meter Grid

	Meter	1	2	3	4	5
A	$\frac{5}{8}$	2+3	3+2			
B	$\frac{7}{8}$	2+2+3	3+2+2	2+3+2		
C	$\frac{8}{8}$	2+3+3	3+2+3	3+3+2		
D	$\frac{11}{8}$	2+3+3+3	3+2+3+3	3+3+2+3	3+3+3+2	
E	$\frac{13}{8}$	2+3+2+3+3	3+2+3+2+3	3+3+2+3+2	2+3+3+2+3	3+2+3+3+2

Mixed Meter   *Exercise 8.2*

Objective: Conduct changing time signatures, keeping
a steady pulse.

1. Conduct with and without accents—without accents first. When you
   conduct with an accent, give the ictus (where the accent occurs) more
   weight and force than normal.

2. Practice with a metronome or an ensemble. For these exercises
   use ♪ = 160.

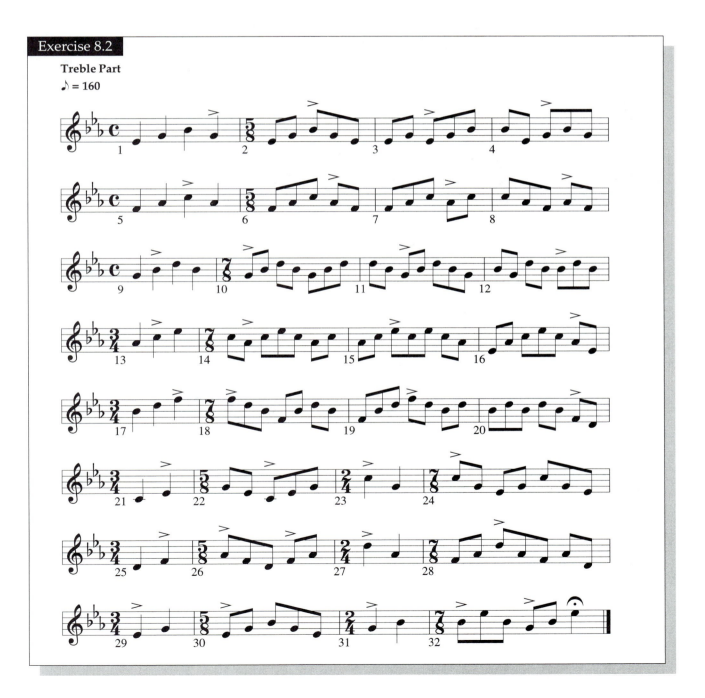

Exercise 8.2

Treble Part

♪ = 160

Exercise 8.2

F Part

♪ = 160

Exercise 8.2

E♭ Part

♪ = 160

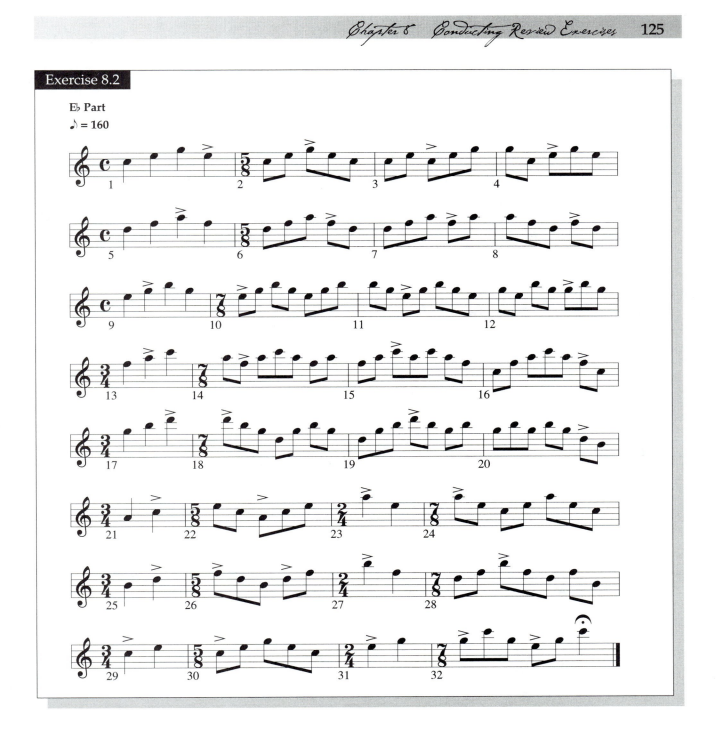

Exercise 8.2

B♭ Part

♪ = 160

Exercise 8.2

Bass Part

♪ = 160

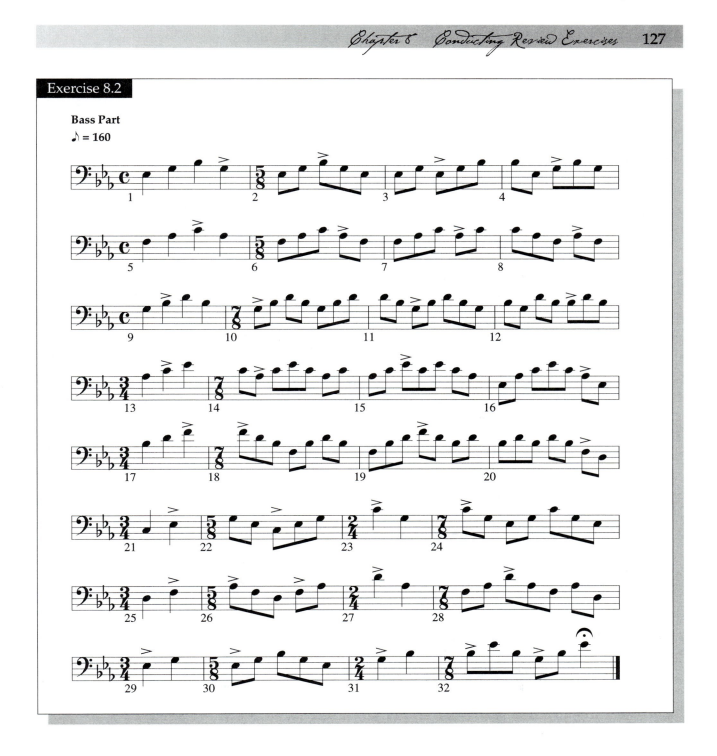

Exercise 8.3   Mixed Meter

Exercise 8.3

Treble Part

♪ = 160

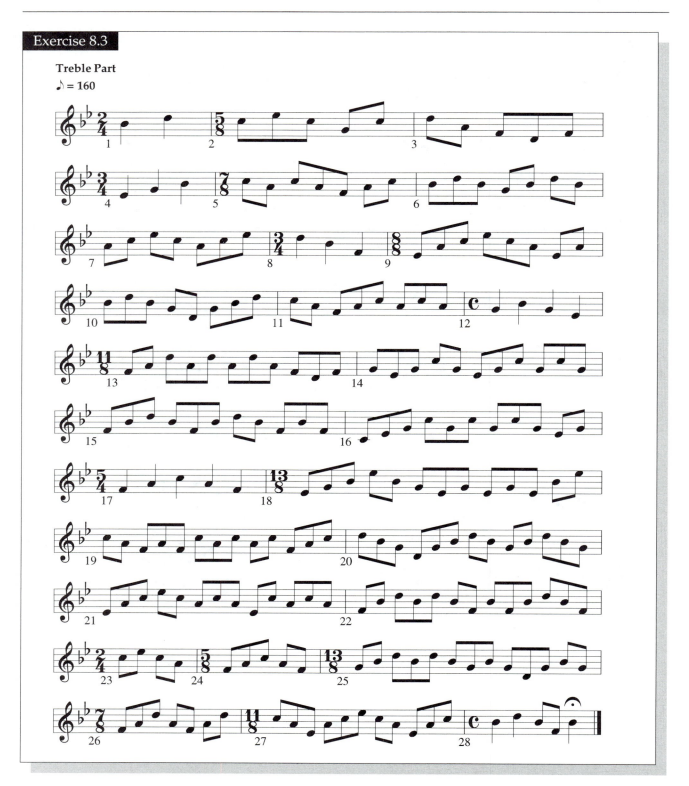

Exercise 8.3

F Part

♪ = 160

Exercise 8.3

E♭ Part

♪ = 160

Exercise 8.3

B♭ Part

♪ = 160

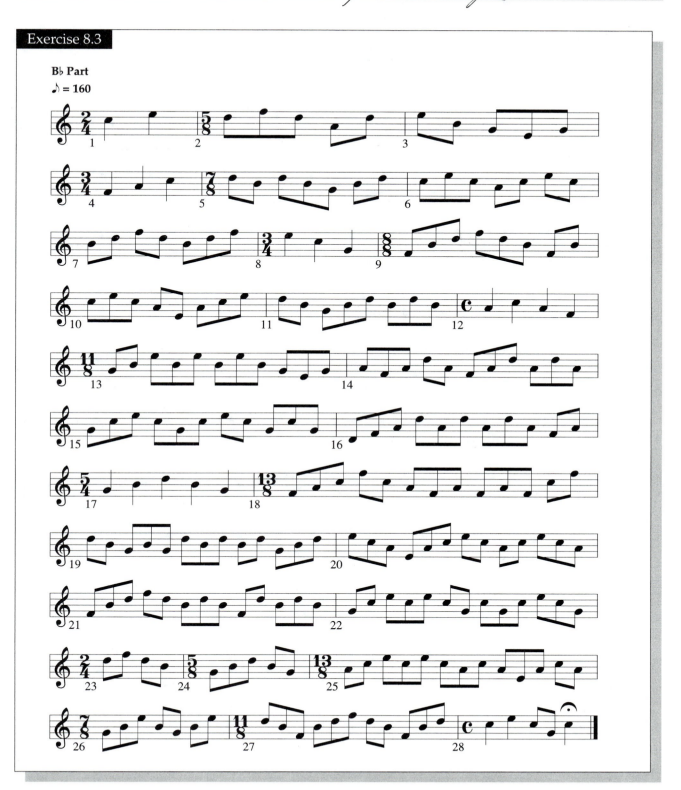

Exercise 8.3

Bass Part

♪ = 160

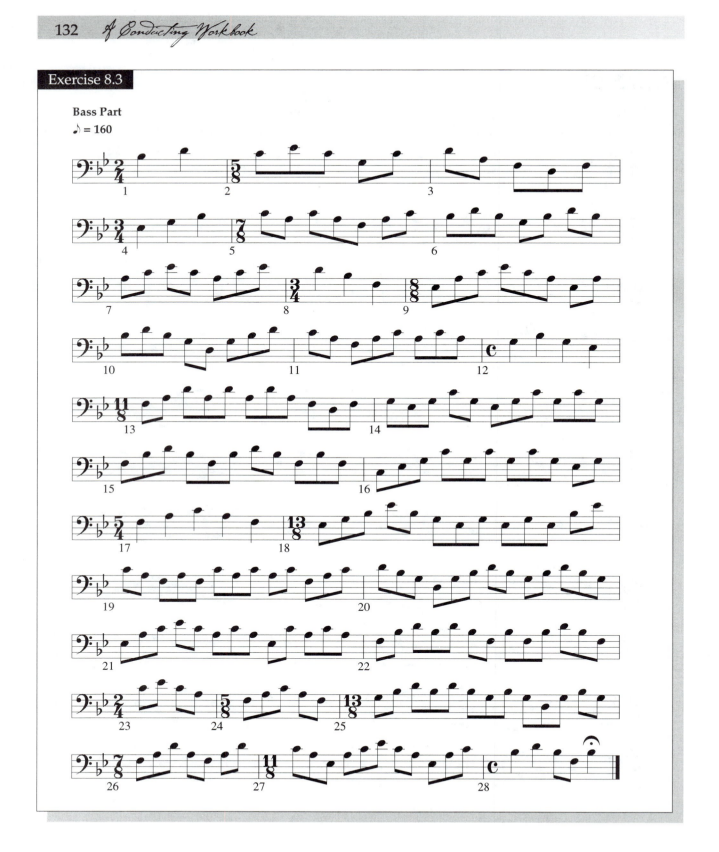

The Grand Staff

The diagram that follows clarifies clef relationships. The tenor clef is very useful for trombonists and bassoonists, and also for cellists who perform in an orchestra and play advanced literature. The alto clef is used occasionally for viola and occasionally for trombonists (it was intended originally for alto trombone) in orchestral literature.

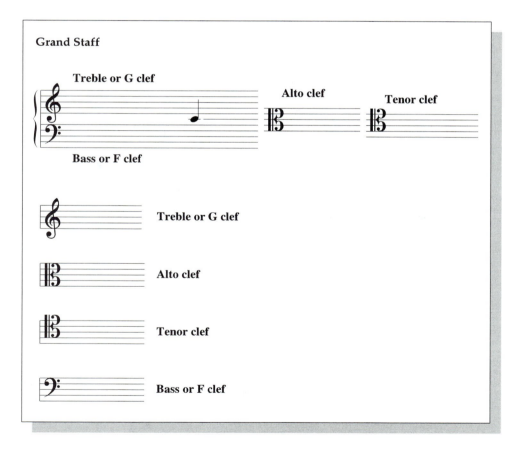

Grand Staff

Treble or G clef

Alto clef

Tenor clef

Bass or F clef

Treble or G clef

Alto clef

Tenor clef

Bass or F clef

Intervals of Transposition

The intervals of transposition are demonstrated by the chart that follows on the next three pages. Transposition is often a problem for young conductors, and it may persist in more mature conductors. Whether transposing a single part or reading a full transposed score, it is imperative that the conductor know and understand intervals of transposition. Unless there is a secure knowledge of the actual pitch coming from each transposing instrument, the conductor is unable to recreate accurately the sound and intent of the composer.

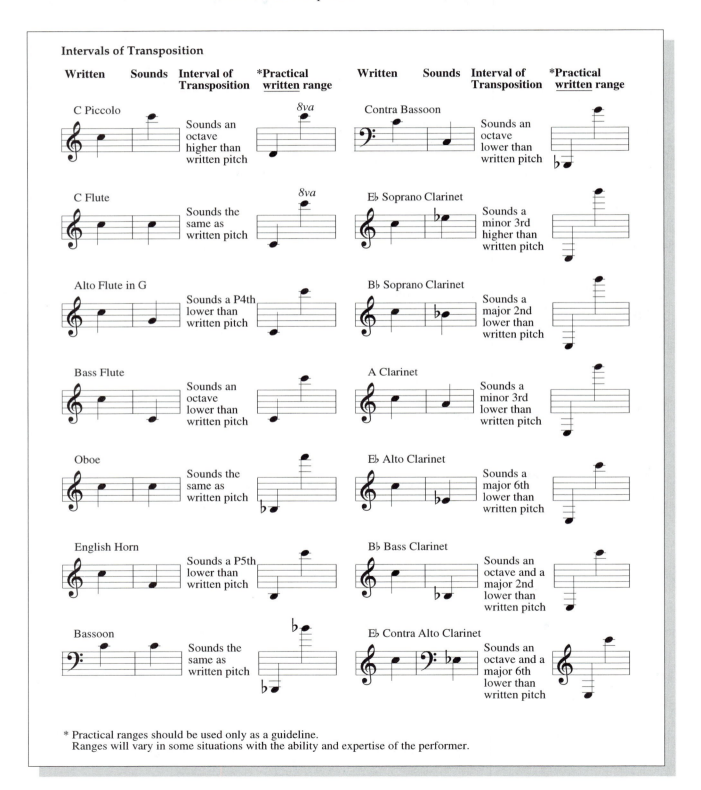

Intervals of Transposition

* Practical ranges should be used only as a guideline.
  Ranges will vary in some situations with the ability and expertise of the performer.

Intervals of Transposition (*continued*)

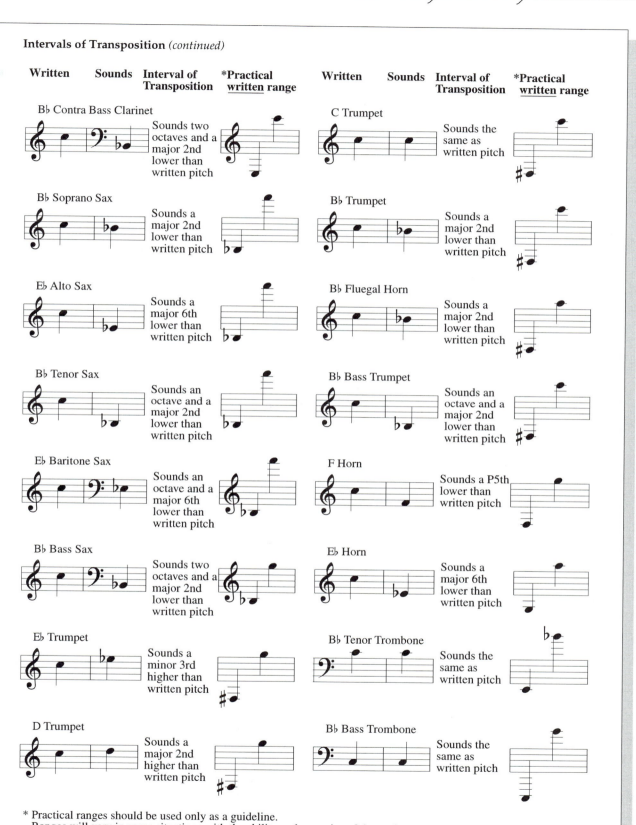

* Practical ranges should be used only as a guideline.
  Ranges will vary in some situations with the ability and expertise of the performer.

Intervals of Transposition (continued)

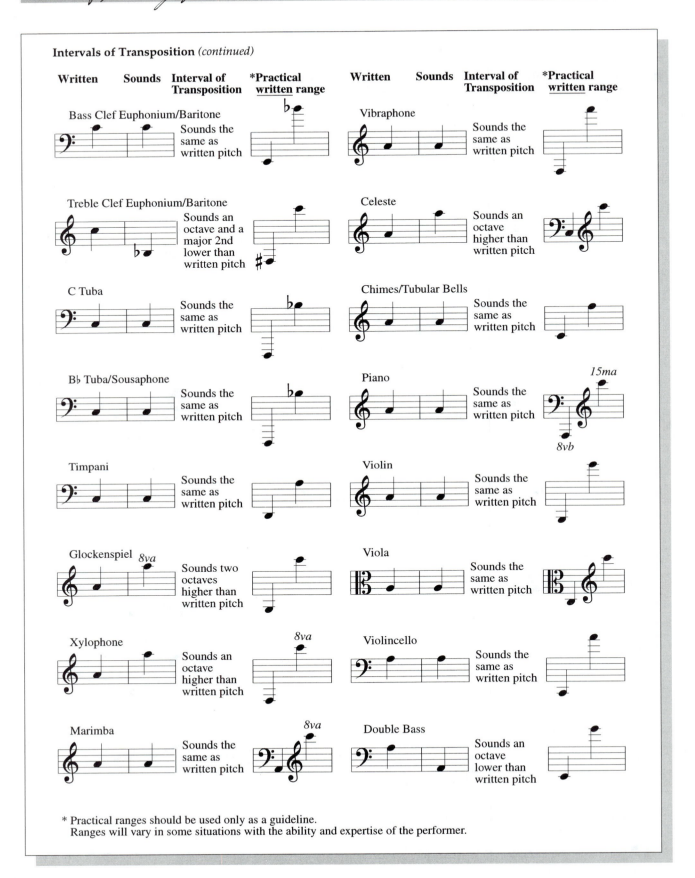

* Practical ranges should be used only as a guideline.
  Ranges will vary in some situations with the ability and expertise of the performer.

The following exercises are designed to help each conductor become comfortable reading a condensed or transposed score. From the condensed score (in concert pitch), the conductor will need to know what transposed note each transposing instrument should play. From the full transposed score (individual parts are written in the score as the players see their part), the conductor will need to know the concert pitch sounding from each transposing instrument.

From Tranposed to Concert Pitch   *Exercise 9.1*

Objective: Show relationship between the transposed pitch (written) and the concert pitch (sound) by notating the concert pitch on the staff provided.

1. For each of the given *transposed* pitches (or *concert* pitches for nontransposing instruments), write the concert pitch for the instrument shown. Include the correct clef, key signature, and accidentals.

2. You are encouraged to write additional exercises.

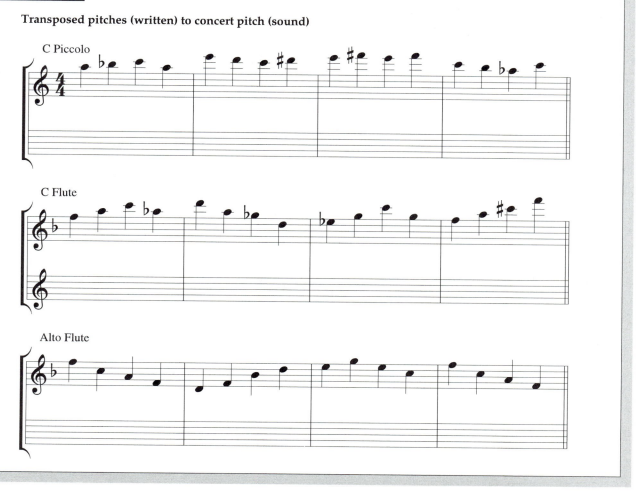

Exercise 9.1

Transposed pitches (written) to concert pitch (sound) *(continued)*

Exercise 9.1

Transposed pitches (written) to concert pitch (sound) *(continued)*

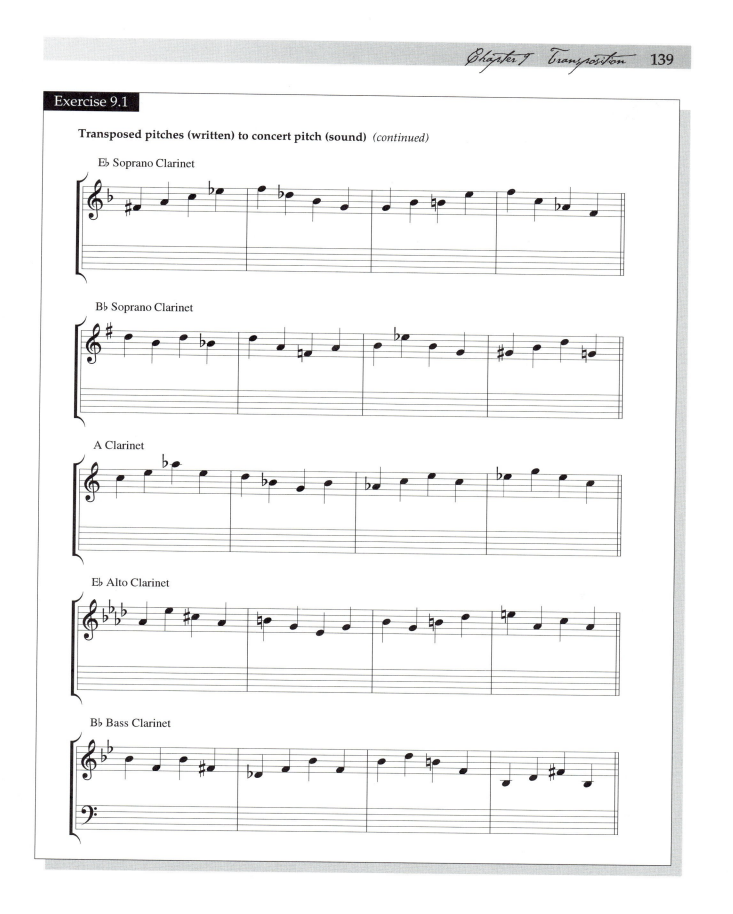

Exercise 9.1

Transposed pitches (written) to concert pitch (sound) *(continued)*

Exercise 9.1

Transposed pitches (written) to concert pitch (sound) *(continued)*

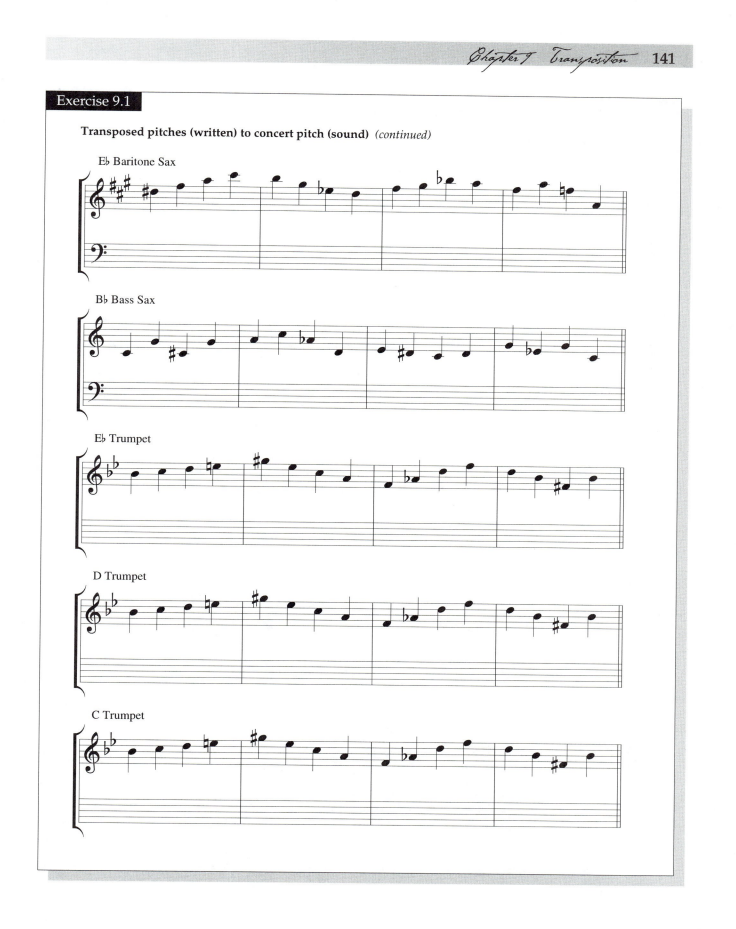

Exercise 9.1

Transposed pitches (written) to concert pitch (sound) *(continued)*

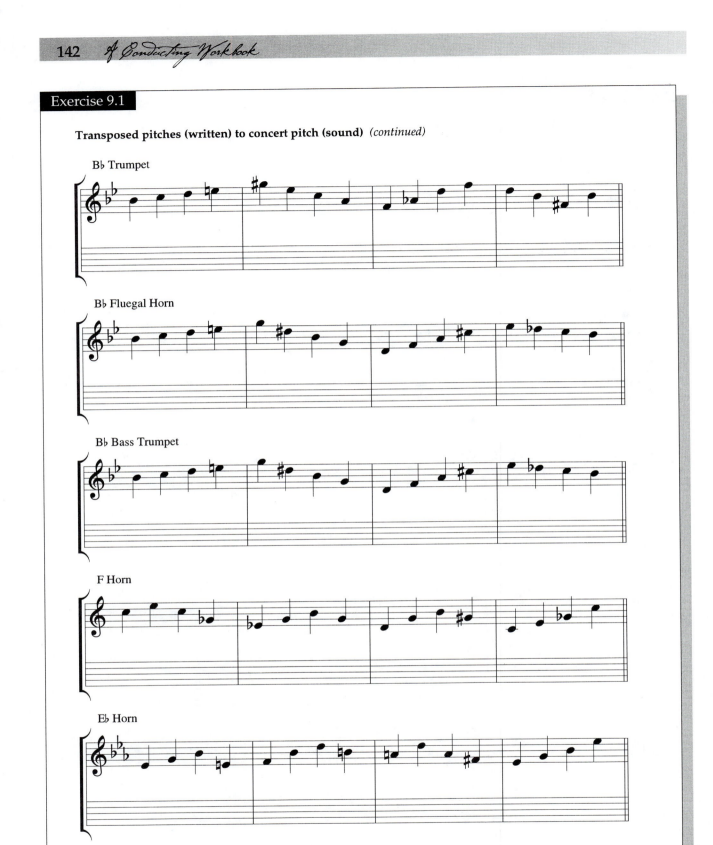

Exercise 9.1

Transposed pitches (written) to concert pitch (sound) *(continued)*

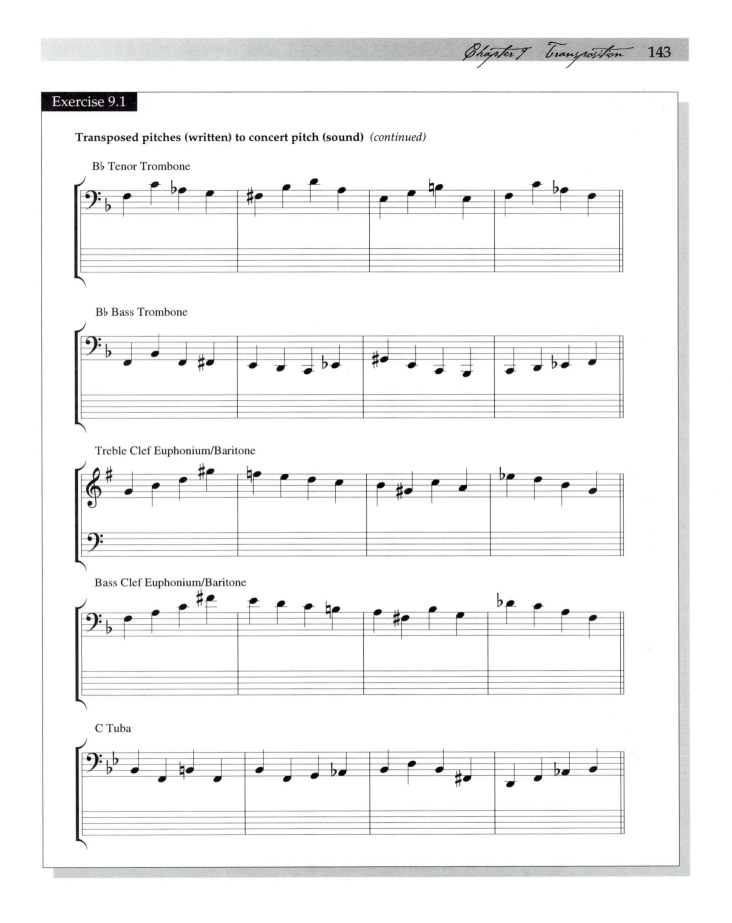

Exercise 9.1

Transposed pitches (written) to concert pitch (sound) *(continued)*

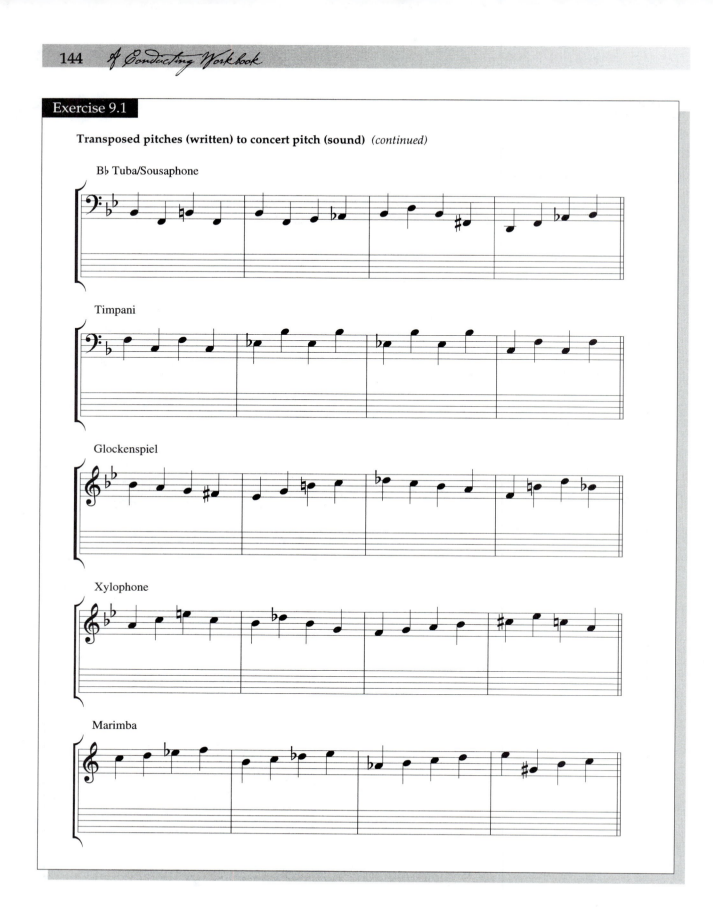

Exercise 9.1

Transposed pitches (written) to concert pitch (sound) *(continued)*

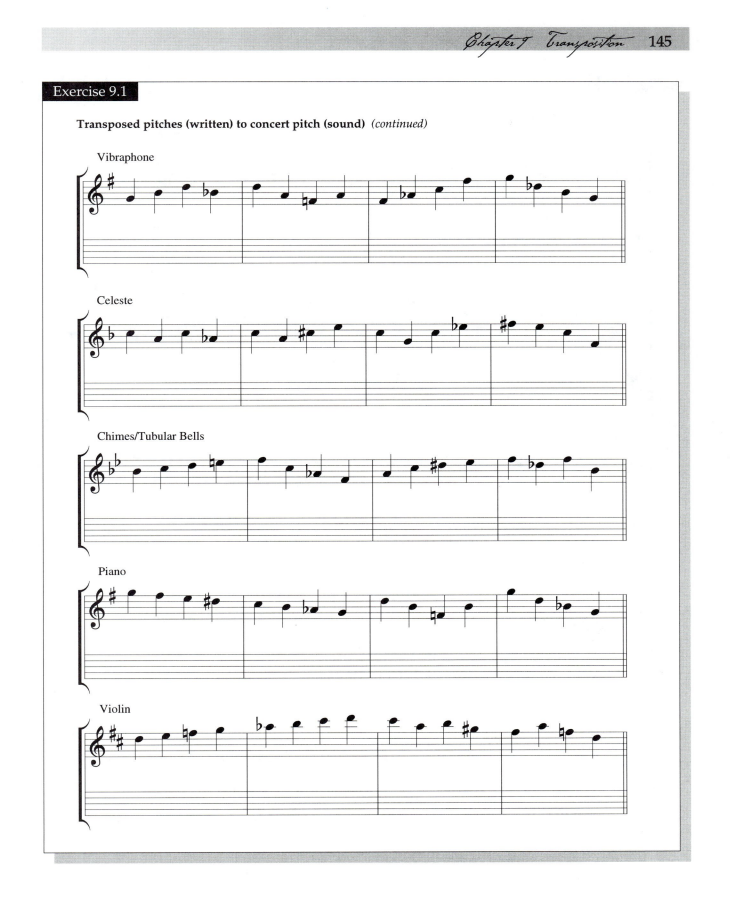

Exercise 9.1

Transposed pitches (written) to concert pitch (sound) *(continued)*

From Concert to Transposed Pitch   *Exercise 9.2*

Objective: Show relationship between the concert pitch (sound) and the transposed pitch (written) by notating the transposed pitch on the staff provided.

1. From the given concert pitches, write a transposed part (if it is a transposing instrument) for the instruments requested. Include correct clef, key signature, and accidentals.

2. You are encouraged to write additional exercises.

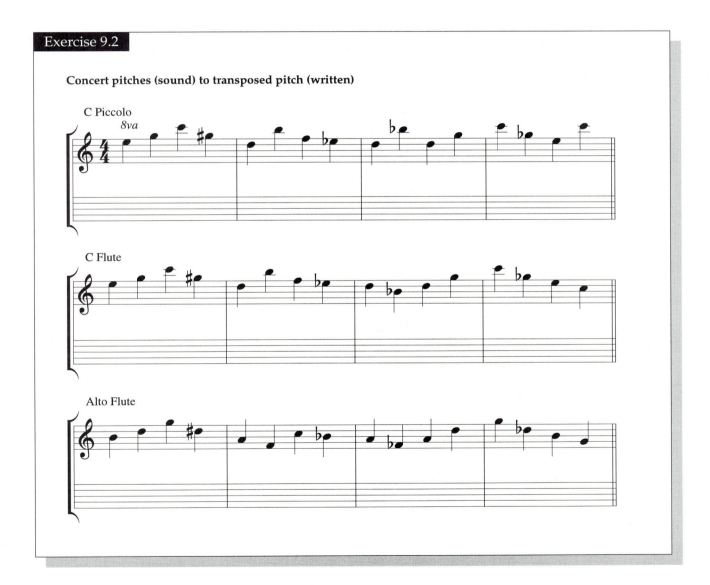

Exercise 9.2

Concert pitches (sound) to transposed pitch (written)

Exercise 9.2

Concert pitches (sound) to transposed pitch (written) (*continued*)

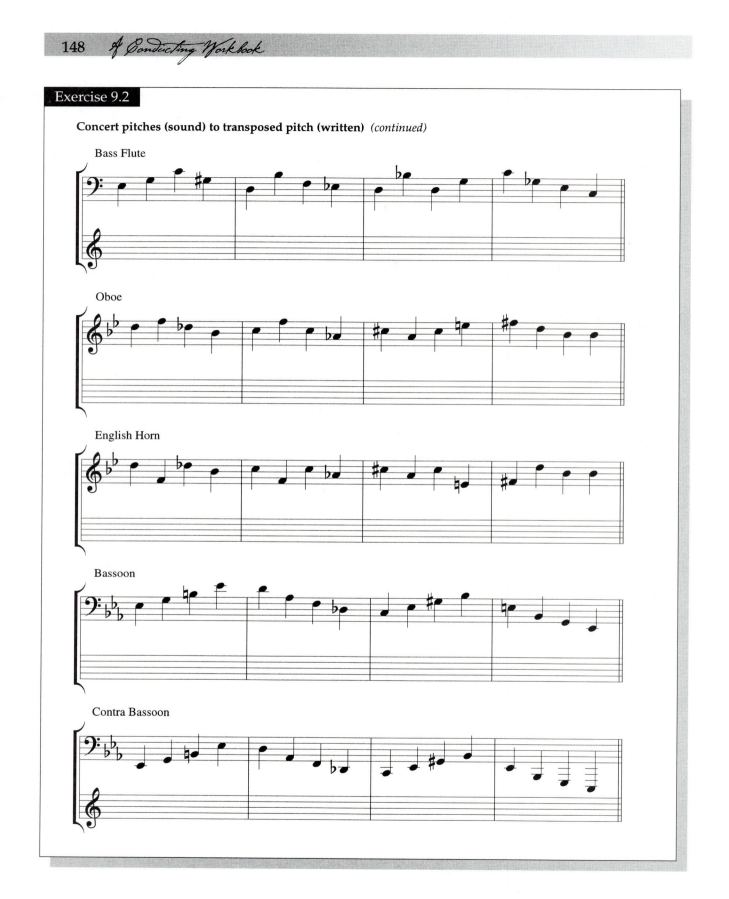

Exercise 9.2

Concert pitches (sound) to transposed pitch (written) *(continued)*

Exercise 9.2

Concert pitches (sound) to transposed pitch (written) *(continued)*

Eb Contra Alto Clarinet

Bb Contra Bass Clarinet

Bb Soprano Sax

Eb Alto Sax

Bb Tenor Sax

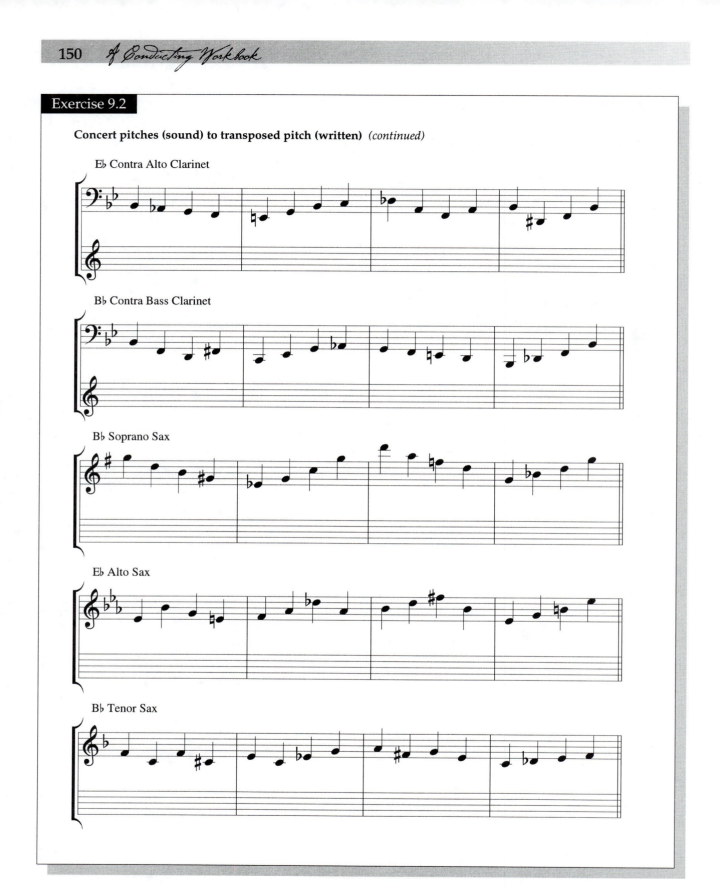

Exercise 9.2

Concert pitches (sound) to transposed pitch (written) *(continued)*

Exercise 9.2

Concert pitches (sound) to transposed pitch (written) *(continued)*

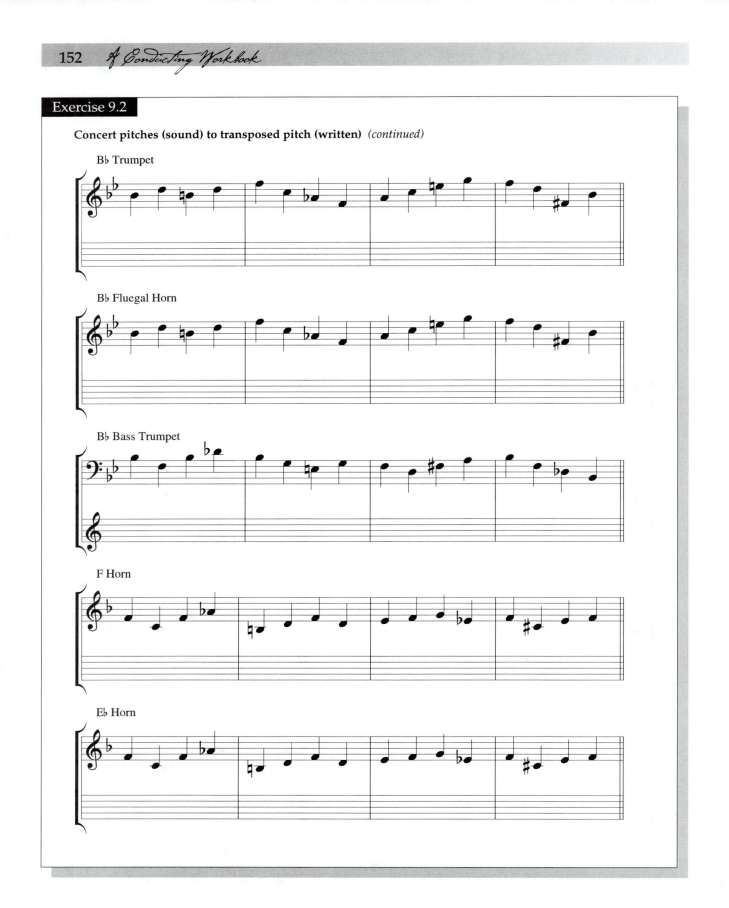

Exercise 9.2

Concert pitches (sound) to transposed pitch (written) *(continued)*

Exercise 9.2

Concert pitches (sound) to transposed pitch (written) *(continued)*

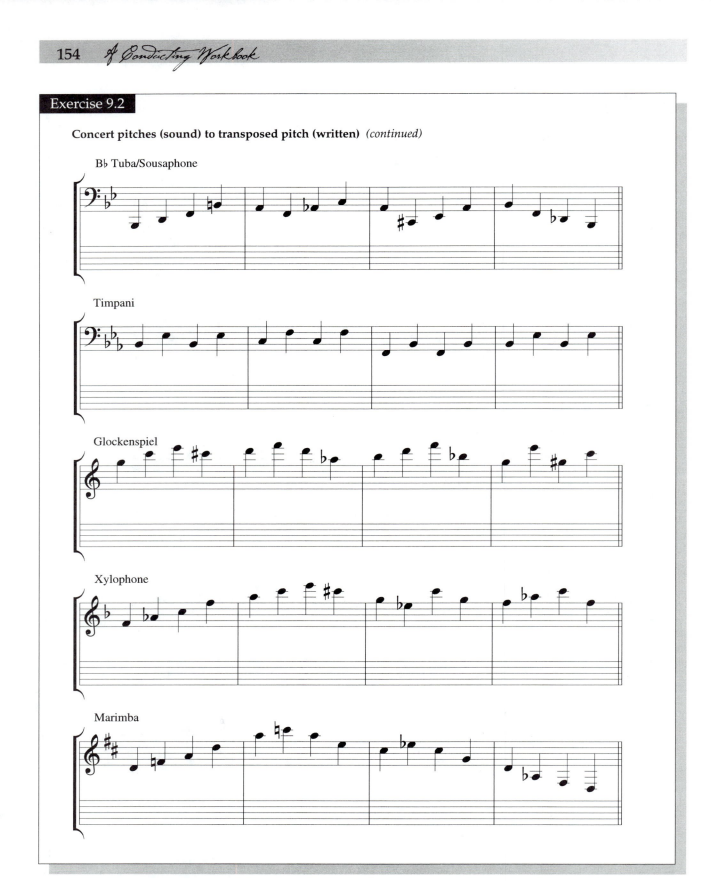

Exercise 9.2

Concert pitches (sound) to transposed pitch (written) *(continued)*

Vibraphone

Celeste

Chimes/Tubular Bells

Piano

Violin

Exercise 9.2

Concert pitches (sound) to transposed pitch (written) *(continued)*

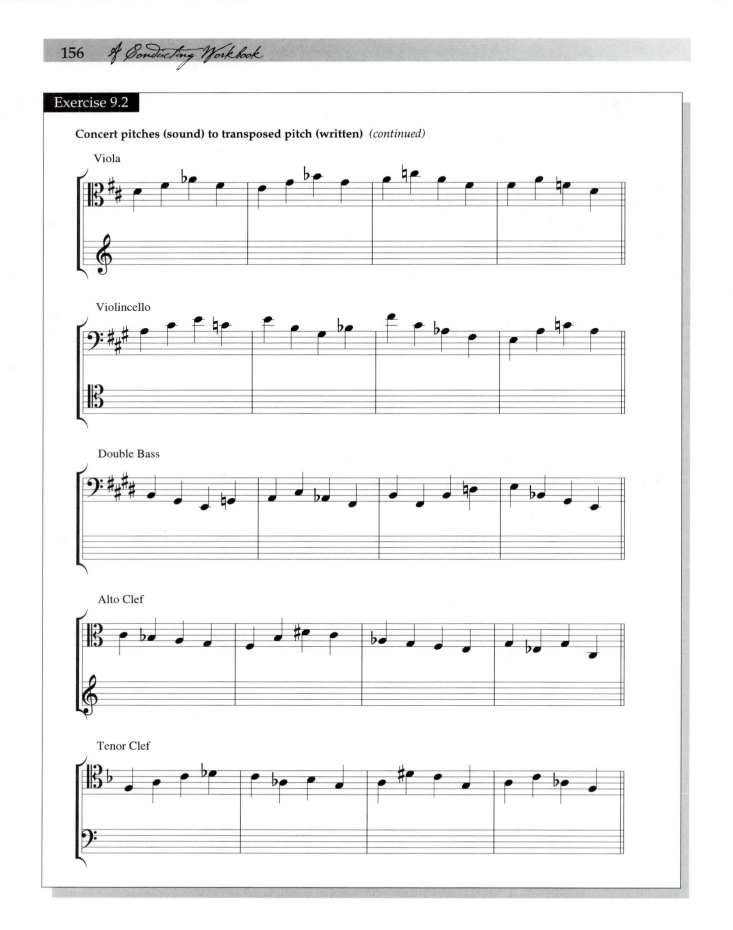

Transposing and Conducting a Brief Chorale

Chorale Arranging   *Exercise 9.3*

Objective: Write a full, transposed score.

1. Arrange one or more of the following chorales, writing a full, transposed score. (This means the parts written in the score are exactly the same as those the players are reading.)

2. For this exercise, *everything* must be correct. If any part is incorrect the arrangement is not acceptable. If you are unsure of your transpositions, range of instruments, or anything related to the assignment, speak with your instructor. Remember, too, that fellow musicians are excellent sources of information.

3. You will need to purchase full-score manuscript paper. Number the measures on the score and on each part. This will facilitate your work and save rehearsal and instruction time.

4. The first assignment should *not* use a computerized music writing program. A computer program may be used after a thorough knowledge of transposition is secure.

5. After completion of the full score, the instructor will indicate if all parts are to be copied and played, or just the parts for the instrumentation of the class.

6. Conduct your arrangement.

Exercise 9.3

Aus meines herzens Grunde

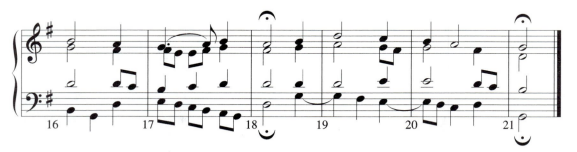

Exercise 9.3

Freuet euch, ihr Christen

Exercise 9.3

Schmucke dich, o liebe Seele

3

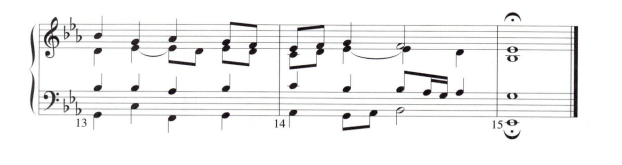

Exercise 9.3

Es spricht der Unweisen Mund

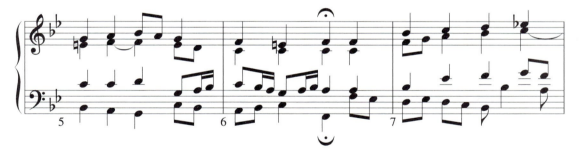

Exercise 9.3

Erbarm'dich mein, o Herre Gott

Exercise 9.3

Mit Fried' und Freud' fahr' ich dahin

Exercise 9.3

Jesu Leiden, Pein und Tod

Exercise 9.3

Christus, der uns selig macht

Exercise 9.3

O grosser Gott von Macht

Exercise 9.3

Ermuntre dich, mein schwacher Geist

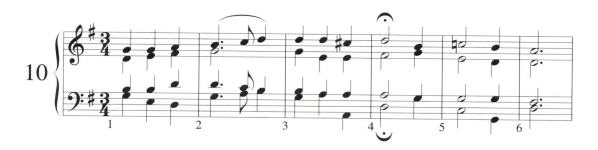

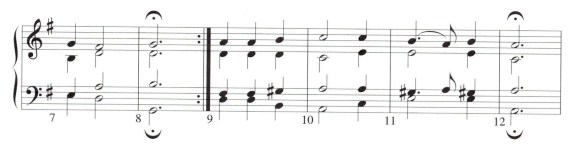

Exercise 9.3

Herzlich lieb hab' ich dich, o Herr

Exercise 9.3

Singen wir aus Herzens Grund

Exercise 9.3

Christus, der uns selig macht

Exercise 9.3

Christ, unser Herr, zum Jordan kam

Exercise 9.3

Ist Gott mein Schild und helfersmann

15

 For additional chorales, go to Web site *http://www.wadsworth.com/music.*

CHAPTER 10

Conducting a Full Score

Preparation

*I*n this chapter you will prepare, rehearse, and conduct a full score. With assistance from your instructor, select a published composition to conduct. *Before* class starts, complete the score study guide that follows and give it to your instructor.

Score Study Guide

Name of Composer

Information about composer

Name of composition

Publication year and publisher

Information about arranger

Composition originally composed for: band, orchestra, voice, piano, other

Length of composition (time) for program building.   Min.   Sec.

Time signature changes

Tempo changes

Style changes: legato, separated, marcato, and so on

Potential pitch problems and solutions

Potential balance problems and solutions

Potential technique problems and solutions

Potential range/tessitura problems and solutions

Potential rhythmic problems and solutions

Potential conducting problems and solutions; fermati, cuing, and so on

Always return music to files in *Score Order.*

Exercise 10.1   Completing a Full Score Reduction Chart

Objectives: (1) Show how parts are doubled, (2) show how a full score can be reduced to basic chord structures, (3) allay some of the trepidation young conductors have in dealing with a full score, and (4) reinforce the issue of transposing parts in the full score.

1. Choose four measures from the full score of the composition you will be conducting and complete the full score reduction chart. Two examples appear in this chapter.

2. You are encouraged to copy the blank full score reduction chart that follows for use with additional measures.

3. Identify the concert (sounding) pitch being played by each instrument, writing it on the staff and in the correct octave.

4. Draw a line from the instrument name to the concert pitch on the staff.

5. Analyze the score after transposing all parts to concert pitch.

Exercise 10.1   **Example for using Full Score Reduction Chart   Example A**

Draw a line from each pitch in the transposed score to the concert pitch being played.

Composition: __Bb Chord__

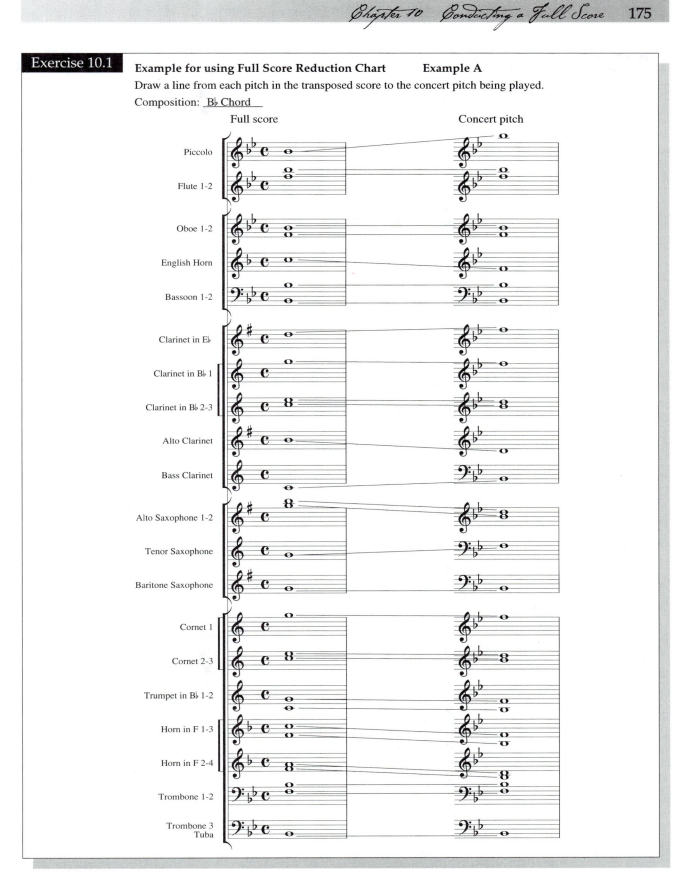

Use this example to generate a form that will help students better understand the transposition of a full score as it related to concert pitch.

Exercise 10.1   **Example for using Full Score Reduction Chart**   **Example B**

Draw a line from each pitch in the transposed score to the concert pitch being played.

Composition: _Bb Chord_

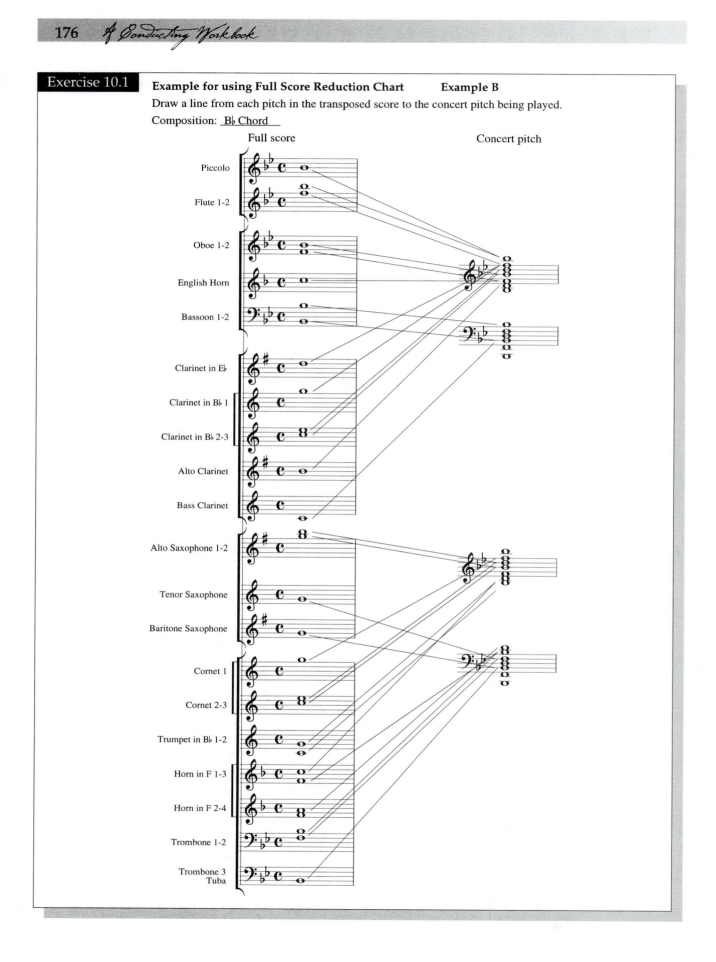

Exercise 10.1

Composition_____

Full Score Reduction Chart
(Copy as needed)

Picc.

Flute

Oboe

Bassoon

E♭ Sop. Cl.

B♭ Cl. I

B♭ Cl. II

B♭ Cl. III

E♭ Alto Cl.

B♭ Bass Cl.

E♭ Contra Alto Cl.

B♭ Contra Bass Cl.

Alto Sax I

Alto Sax II

Tenor Sax

Bari. Sax

Trpt. I

Trpt. II

Trpt. III

Hn. I

Hn. II

Hn. III

Hn. IV

Trb. I

Trb. II

Trb. III

Euphonium

Tuba

Percussion

Exercise 10.1

Composition_____

Full score

Piccolo

Flute 1-2

Oboe 1-2

English Horn

Bassoon 1-2

Clarinet in E♭

Clarinet in B♭ 1

Clarinet in B♭ 2-3

Alto Clarinet

Bass Clarinet

Alto Saxophone 1-2

Tenor Saxophone

Baritone Saxophone

Cornet 1

Cornet 2-3

Trumpet in B♭ 1-2

Horn in F 1-3

Horn in F 2-4

Trombone 1-2

Trombone 3
Tuba

Full Score Reduction Chart
(Copy as needed)

Concert pitch

The Rehearsal

The Conductor as Benevolent Dictator

In view of the myriad details a conductor must consider during a rehearsal, all conductors might do well to remember the truth of the maxim "Conducting is a privilege." The musical and emotional interaction between the conductor and members of the ensemble is an important issue in the dynamics of every rehearsal. While many conductors profess that music-making is a collaborative effort (and it is), the fact remains that the conductor is the leader and a dictator of sorts. Someone must make the final decisions about the selection of the music, its interpretation, and the expectation levels of the performance, in concert and in rehearsal, and that person is the conductor. Some conductors profess to other conductors that they are benevolent toward their ensembles, in the sense that a "benevolent dictator" is capable of expressing honest musical values and preparing to the best of his abilities. Such a conductor must also be able to establish a rapport with the ensemble that is based on respect for each individual and for the music.

Problem Solving

A fine conductor has the ability to detect and correct problems in the ensemble's music-making during rehearsal. *Do not assume anything; leave nothing to chance; study the score.* The conductor must have an aural sense about what the composer intended for the composition. Studying the score, using the piano, listening to recordings, or playing individual parts on your instrument are excellent starting points. The conductor must know the harmonic, rhythmic, and melodic structure of the composition well enough to identify incorrect harmonies, rhythms, and melodies. Without the ability to identify and correct mistakes during a rehearsal, the ensemble may be producing sound, but sound that does not reflect the composer's intent.

Ensemble Integrity

Starting the first sounds together seems to be a problem in many ensembles. If this problem occurs during a concert, it can usually be traced back to the rehearsal. Spending time working so that the ictus of the initial sound is together will not only set the stage for the rest of the rehearsal but will also ensure a secure foundation for the concert performance. Once the composition has started, the challenge of staying together does not seem to be as great.

A technique that helps produce a solid ensemble sound is to ask all players who play a certain melodic, harmonic, or rhythmic line to isolate and play that part together. It often comes as a surprise to some ensemble members that they are playing the same part or rhythm as a player fifty feet away in a different section of the ensemble. It is often difficult for a player to hear, much less know, which instruments share the same part.

A conductor must maintain integrity not only in the music's horizontal flow but also in the vertical, harmonic sound of the score, the rhythm, and the rhythmic pulse. An effective way to produce solid chordal sounds or harmonies is to ask the ensemble to play *as chords* those areas that do not have musical chordal integrity—for example, the "stinger" at the end of a march. The final note of a march is often thrown away, and neither the conductor, the ensemble, nor the audience hears the final note as a chord. Ask the ensemble to play the final note as a chord and to hold the note for a few seconds. Next, ask the ensemble to play the final note in time but retain the sound of the chord. There will be many members of the ensemble who have never heard the sound of a chord on that particular note. This technique may be used successfully for phrase endings and pick-up notes that require a full ensemble sound. (I use the term *full ensemble sound* when all ensemble members are playing the same rhythm at the same time.)

Dynamics

The proper use of dynamics can be a major problem in an ensemble's performance. The starting point is, of course, on the printed page, but what is the time period of the composition? The dynamic levels used in the Classical time period would probably not be appropriate for a composition from the twenty-first century full of percussion and heavy brass. With the cooperation of the performers, the conductor can help the musicians understand the intent of the composer and how to achieve the best dynamic and musical results.

Proper dynamics relate directly to the balance within the ensemble. Common sense must prevail when balancing parts and sections. A trumpet part marked *forte* in the upper register needs to balance against the clarinet part marked *forte* in the lower register. Most often the challenge for an ensemble is to play softly enough to make effective musical contrasts. It is often more difficult to play softly and slowly than to play a constant *mezzoforte*. Using chorales as warm-up material (or at some point in the rehearsal) can help an ensemble achieve control while playing softly.

Effective Rehearsal Techniques

1. As the conductor, have a written list of items you want to accomplish during every rehearsal.

2. At the beginning, or during, each rehearsal tune individuals or sections, but *tune.*

3. Work for the correct balance of parts within each section and the correct balance among sections.

4. Constantly ask for the best *quality* sound each player can produce.

5. Constantly ask for the best *intonation* each player can produce. Asking the band to sing chorales or band parts is an excellent way to improve intonation.

6. While conducting, *do not sing or hum* a part in the score. When you sing or hum a part, you will not be able to hear what the ensemble is actually playing.

7. Start a tape recorder/video camera when the bell rings for the beginning of rehearsal. Stop the tape/video when the bell or clock signals the end of rehearsal. Taping will clarify how much time you actually spend working on music, demonstrate whether you are talking too much, and give you the opportunity to observe a variety of other rehearsal problems. Tape recording or video taping your rehearsals will usually produce better final results with your ensemble. Try using the accompanying tracking chart to gain greater insight into your rehearsals.

8. Use a numbering system (see the sample charts in the Appendix) on all concert and marching band music.

9. Have chairs and stands in place before students enter the rehearsal room.

10. Add to this list the techniques that work best for you.

Tracking the Rehearsal

Class period _____ Time _____ Director _____

Time	Activity	Results or Comments
	From bell to all playing warm-up	
	Tuning	
	Sight Reading	
	Other compositions	

Conducting a Published Composition

Exercise 10.2   *Conducting Published Music*

1. *Before* class starts, place individual parts of your selected published composition in individual folders. This will save rehearsal time.

2. Rehearse together the parts that are in unison or octaves.

3. Rehearse together the parts with the same rhythm.

4. Observe tessitura of all instruments.

5. Observe ranges of all instruments.

6. Observe how smoothly (voice leadings) each part is written for each instrument.

7. As you rehearse, check for intonation, quality of sound, and balance.

8. As you conduct, be cognizant of good conducting patterns, cuing, dynamic indications, facial expression, body language, and energy.

CHAPTER 11

Advanced Conducting Techniques

Rubato

*R*ubato means "stolen time." Conducting, playing or singing in a rubato style give an emotional impact to music. As a conductor, the places in the music where you choose to slow, then move forward, will have a great impact not only on your musicians but also on the audience. Rubato was not considered a desirable trait in the Classical era, but with the rise of Romantic music rubato came to be used in all types of music; we now hear it in everything from the great Romantic symphonies to the latest pop hits. How and where you choose to effect a rubato style will give an indication to other musicians of your own musicality. The exercises and diagram of this chapter will help you to conduct in a rubato style.

Rubato Preparation   *Exercise 11.1*

Objective: Increase awareness of rubato in your conducting.

1. Place both hands at your sides, with fingers pointing toward the floor and palms facing backward. Slowly raise both hands straight above your head and then lower them; do this several times. Your hands should move as if they are being drawn through water.

2. Place your hands in front of you at waist level, palms facing you with fingertips touching. Using the same kind of motion as before, pull your hands away from each other and back several times. Again, your hands should move as if being drawn through water.

3. Slowly move your hands up and down several times, from each ictus point in the following time signatures: $\frac{2}{4}, \frac{3}{4}, \frac{4}{4}$.

4. Place the baton in your hand. Stop briefly at each ictus point, then slowly raise the baton to the top of the rebound and stop briefly. See the accompanying diagram.

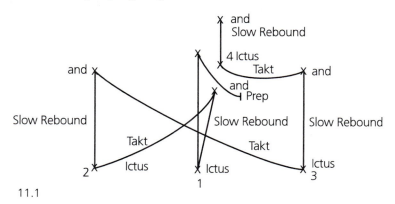

11.1

Exercise 11.2   Rubato

Objective: Work toward musical expression within a note, measure, or musical phrase.

Give the rubato a little extra time by elongating the part of the pattern that includes the rubato note, measure, or phrase. For this exercise, use ♩ = 84.

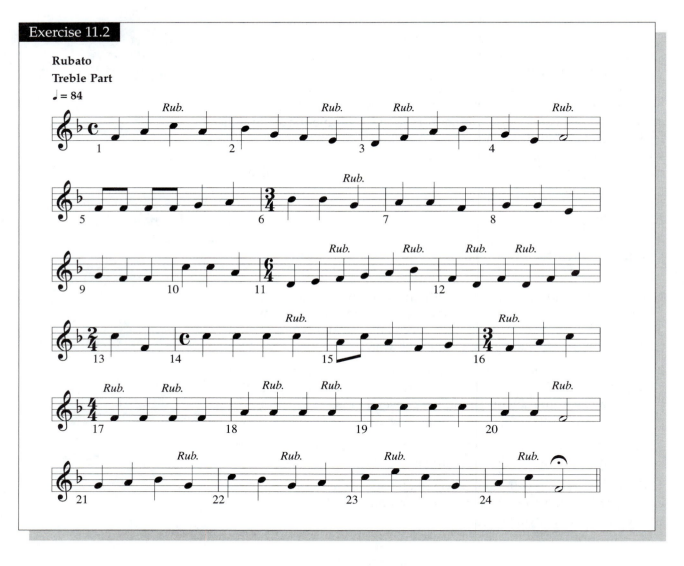

Exercise 11.2

Rubato

F Part

♩ = 84

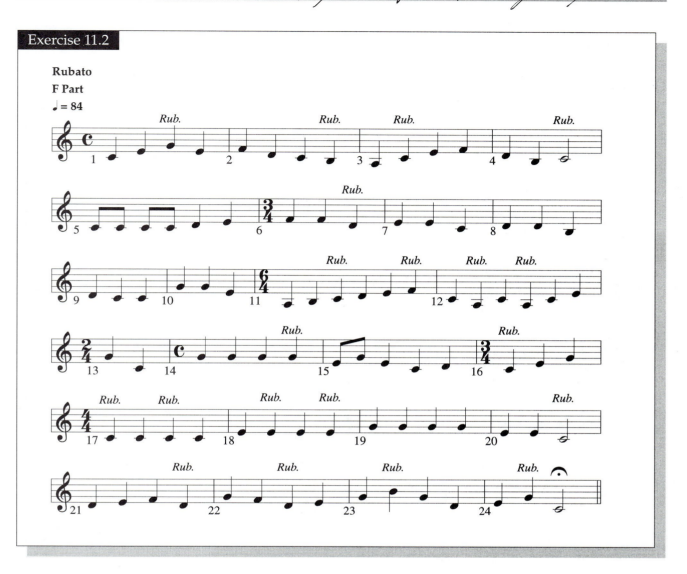

Exercise 11.2

Rubato

E♭ Part

♩ = 84

Exercise 11.2

Rubato

B♭ Part

♩ = 84

Exercise 11.2

Rubato

Bass Part

♩ = 84

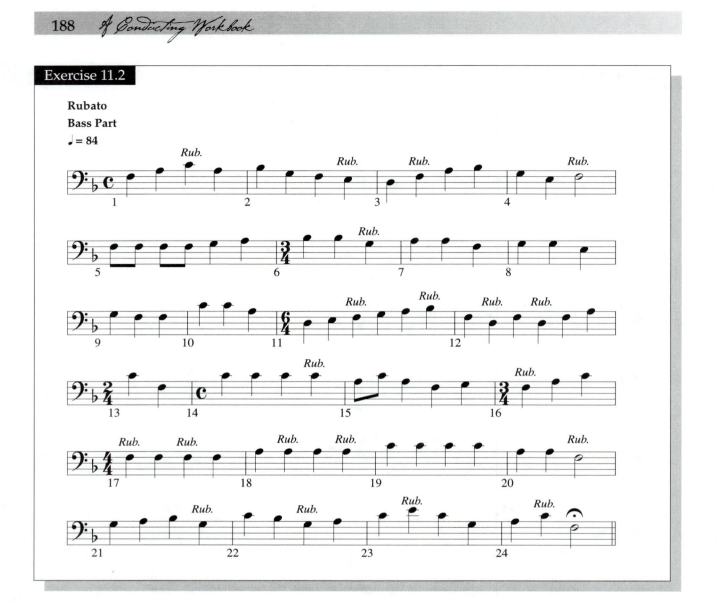

Exercise 11.3   Rubato

Objective: Work toward musical expression within a note, measure, or musical phrase.

Give the rubato a little extra time by elongating the part of the pattern that includes the rubato note, measure, or phrase. For this exercise, use ♩ = 84.

Exercise 11.3

Exercise 11.3

Exercise 11.3

Rubato

E♭ Part

♩ = 84

Exercise 11.3

Rubato

B♭ Part

♩ = 84

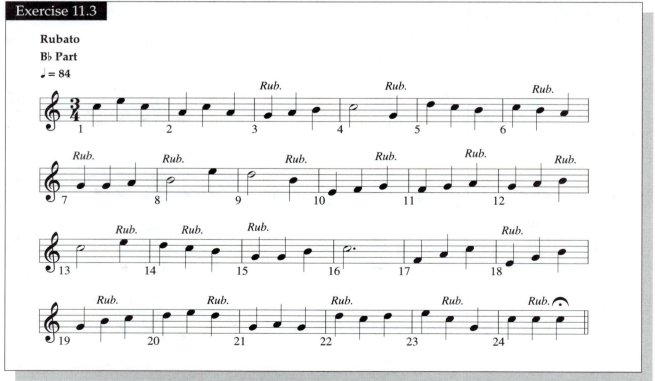

Exercise 11.3

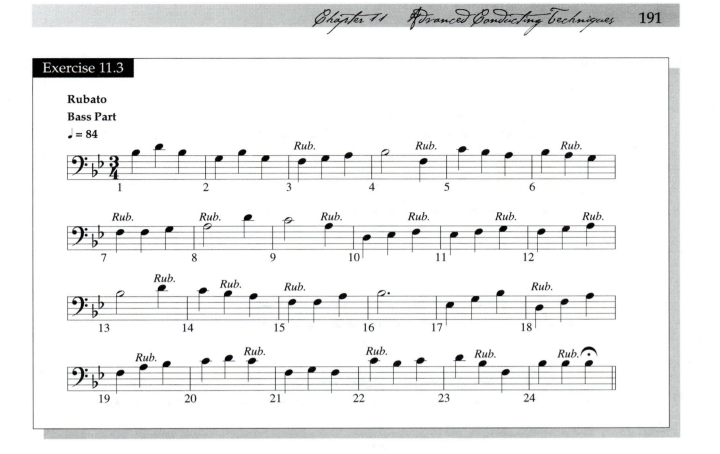

Accelerando and Ritardando

The exercises below address the need to conduct smooth accelerandos and ritards. *Before* conducting the following exercises, the teacher (or student) should choose a time signature. Begin by conducting to a metronome set at ♩ = 80, then gradually move the metronome from 80 to 120 and back to 80. Feel free to use other tempo markings.

Accelerando and Ritardando   *Exercise 11.4*

Objective: Make a smooth, even transition from a slow tempo to a faster tempo and back to a slow tempo.

1. For this nonmelodic exercise, select any major or minor scale.

2. Play a different scale step for each measure of each exercise.

3. Repeat the top note of the scale.

Exercise 11.4

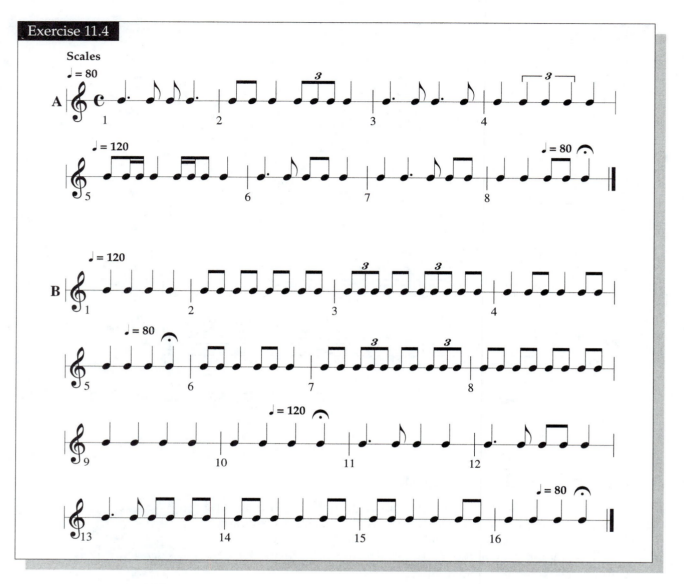

Accelerando and Ritardando

Exercise 11.5

Objective: Make a smooth, even transition from a slow tempo to a faster tempo and back to a slow tempo.

Conduct the music in this melodic exercise by *gradually* increasing the tempo from ♩ = 80 to ♩ = 120, and then *gradually* decreasing the tempo from ♩ = 120 to ♩ = 80.

Exercise 11.5

Accelerando and Ritardando

F Part

Exercise 11.5

Accelerando and Ritardando

E♭ Part

Exercise 11.5

Accelerando and Ritardando

B♭ Part

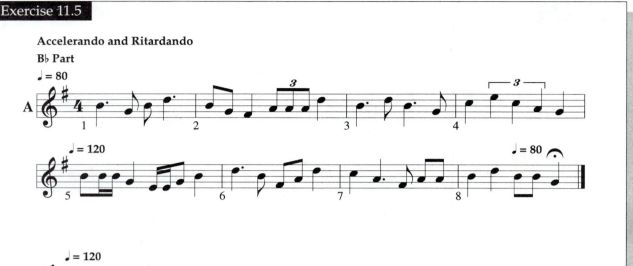

Exercise 11.5

Accelerando and Ritardando

Bass Part

Exercise 11.6   Arranging

Objective: Understand transposition, voice leadings, cross-cuing, doubling of parts, range, and tessitura of instruments.

1. Using the scales chosen in Exercise 11.4, harmonize the scale.

2. Use the harmonized scale to create a full score.

3. Extract parts for the instruments in the class or for all the instruments found in a full score.

Subdivision

Subdivision is most often used with very slow tempos when a basic pattern becomes too cumbersome to clarify the pulse. Subdivision may also be used to clarify a cadence during a ritard. For example, when the resolution occurs on the last eighth note of a measure, subdividing the last beat shows exactly where the resolution occurs.

It may be helpful to think of the subdivided pattern as reconducting each ictus point—which is demonstrated in the accompanying conducting patterns.

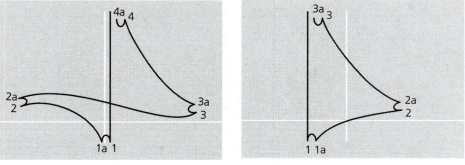

11.2A   11.2B

Subdividing a Single Line   *Exercise 11.7*

Objective: Subdivide a single line in $\frac{3}{4}$ time.

1. Use a subdivided pattern.

2. Vary the tempo markings ($\flat$ = 70).

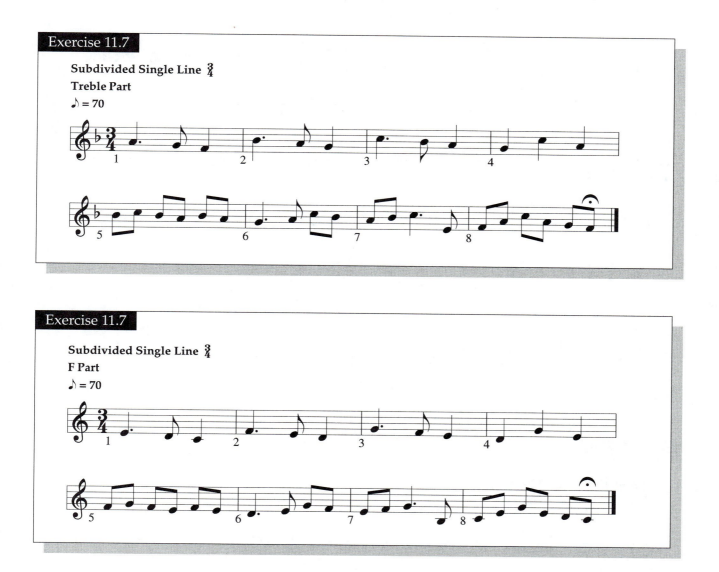

Exercise 11.7

Subdivided Single Line $\frac{3}{4}$

E♭ Part

♪ = 70

Exercise 11.7

Subdivided Single Line $\frac{3}{4}$

B♭ Part

♪ = 70

Exercise 11.7

Subdivided Single Line $\frac{3}{4}$

Bass Part

♪ = 70

Subdividing a Single Line

Objective: Subdivide a single line in $\frac{4}{4}$ time.

1. Use a subdivided pattern.

2. Vary the tempo markings ($\eighthnote$ = 70).

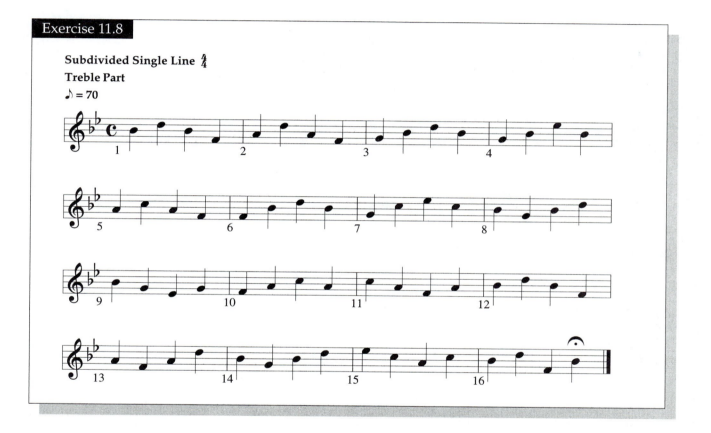

Exercise 11.8

Subdivided Single Line 4/4

F Part

♪ = 70

Exercise 11.8

Subdivided Single Line 4/4

E♭ Part

♪ = 70

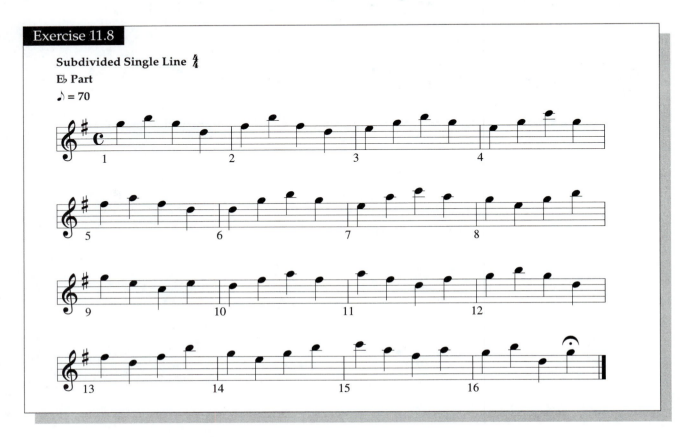

Exercise 11.8

Subdivided Single Line 4/4
B♭ Part
♪ = 70

Exercise 11.8

Subdivided Single Line 4/4
Bass Part
♪ = 70

Exercise 11.9   *Subdividing Harmony*

Objective: Subdivide harmonized in $\frac{3}{4}$ and $\frac{4}{4}$ time.

1. Use a subdivided beat pattern.

2. Select a part appropriate for your instrument and transpose if necessary.

3. Vary the tempo markings (♪ = 70).

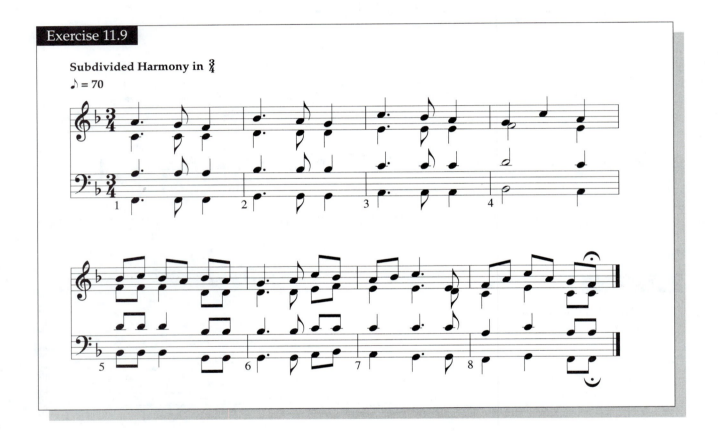

Exercise 11.9

Subdivided Harmony in $\frac{3}{4}$

♪ = 70

Exercise 11.9

Subdivided Harmony in 𝄴

♪ = 70

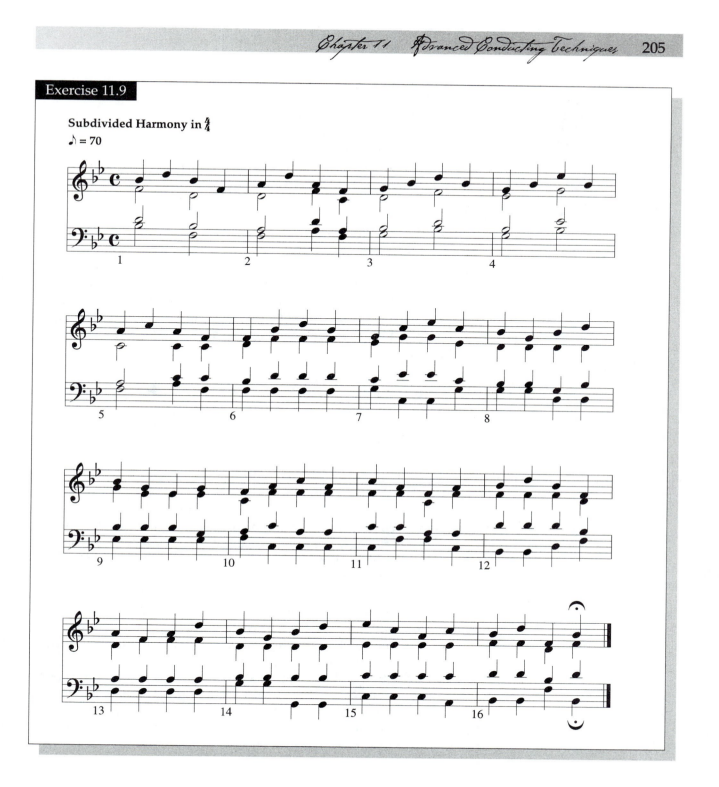

Melding

To meld means to blend or unite. In conducting, *melding* refers to changing the pulse or feel of a measure by changing the conducting pattern in each measure. One example is to change from conducting a waltz in three to conducting one pulse per measure—while keeping the speed of the quarter note constant. When some conductors conduct a melded three-pattern in one pulse to the measure, they jerk the baton away from the ictus point and cause the rebound immediately to rise up to, or above, the head of the conductor. To the conductor, this pattern has a good feel—but it does not indicate counts two and three.

Although it is more difficult for the conductor, I suggest trying the pattern in the accompanying diagrams. Start with a slow tempo, giving each beat of a melded-three an exact position, as shown in the pattern. I believe this pattern will give greater stability to your melded-one pattern and give your musicians a more accurate pattern to read. The diagrams show a side view of the baton.

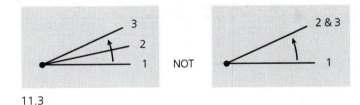

11.3

Another example of melding is to change from conducting four beats per measure to conducting two beats per measure—while keeping the speed of the quarter note constant. Some fast circus marches are easier to conduct if given one pulse per measure as opposed to conducting two beats per measure. Melding is normally used with *allegro* tempi.

The physical advantage of melding for the conductor is to reduce drastically the arm movement needed to conduct an *allegro* tempo. The musical consideration is that the music nearly always seems to have a more melodic, musical flow. For this reason, melding may also be used at slow tempos to create a more sensitive flow to the music.

The construction of the music will dictate the movements of the baton. For example, when conducting at a slow tempo, start conducting in four, then meld into a two pulse. Keep the basic four-pattern, but soften the ictus on counts two and four. Show a more definite ictus on counts one and three, as in the accompanying diagram.

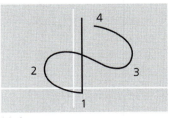

11.4

Melding in a slow three-tempo may also result in a better musical flow. Try the pattern of the following diagrams for a softer approach to the basic three-pattern.

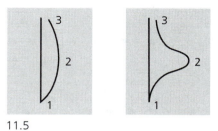

11.5

Melding in a slow $\frac{6}{8}$ tempo may also result in a better musical flow. Using a slower version of the loop two-pattern, shown in the following diagram, works well. (See other conducting patterns in Chapter 2.)

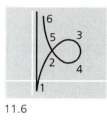

11.6

The following exercises are designed to help achieve a smooth transition from conducting *allegro* into a melded pattern. There is no right or wrong place to change the pattern; each student will quickly find the measure that works best to make the change.

Melding with Scales   *Exercise 11.10*

Objective: Train the muscles and mind to make a smooth transition from conducting a basic time pattern to melding into a different pulse.

Choose any major or minor scale. Play one scale step per measure.

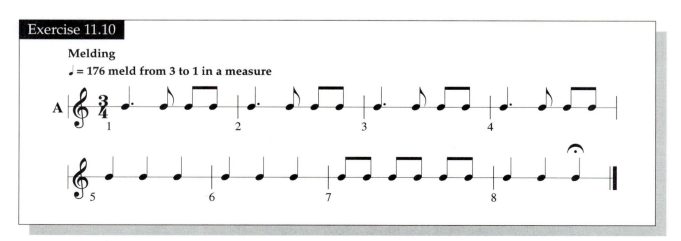

Exercise 11.10

Melding

♩ = 152 meld from 4 to 2 in a measure

Exercise 11.11   Melding in Parts

Exercise 11.11

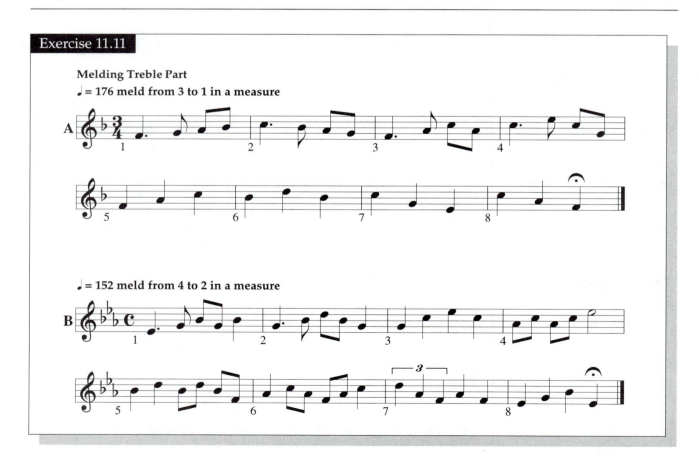

Melding Treble Part

♩ = 176 meld from 3 to 1 in a measure

♩ = 152 meld from 4 to 2 in a measure

Exercise 11.11

Melding Bb Part

♩ = 176 meld from 3 to 1 in a measure

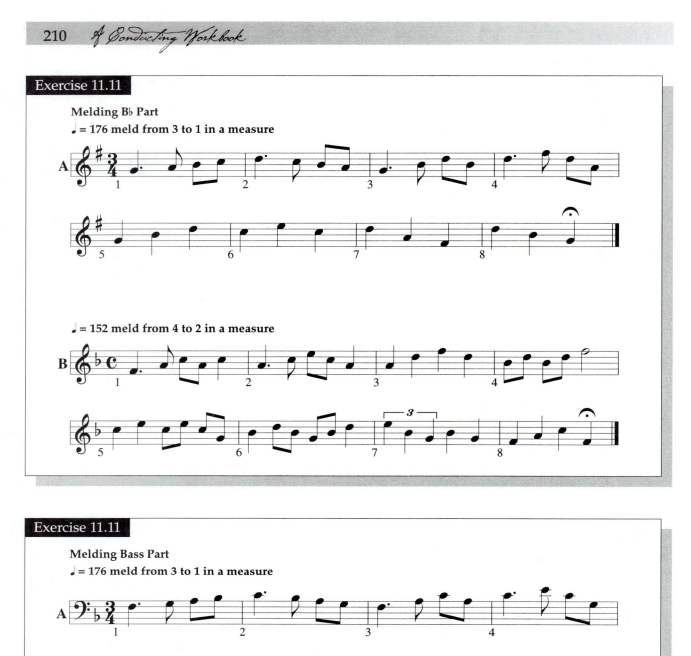

♩ = 152 meld from 4 to 2 in a measure

Exercise 11.11

Melding Bass Part

♩ = 176 meld from 3 to 1 in a measure

♩ = 152 meld from 4 to 2 in a measure

Melding in ¾ Time

Exercise 11.12

1. Start each exercise at ♩ = 100, then accelerate to to ♩ = 160. Meld into one pulse per measure before (but no later than) measure eight.

2. Start each exercise at ♩ = 160. *You* decide when you will change to one pulse per measure.

Exercise 11.12

Melding ¾ Treble Part

♩ = 160

Exercise 11.12

Melding ¾ F Part

♩ = 160

Exercise 11.12

Melding 3/4 Eb Part

♩ = 160

Exercise 11.12

Melding ¾ B♭ Part

♩ = 160

Exercise 11.12

Melding 3/4 Bass Part

♩ = 160

Exercise 11.13   Melding in $\frac{4}{4}$ Time

1. Start each exercise at ♩ = 100, then accelerate to to ♩ = 160. Meld into two pulses per measure before (but no later than) measure eight.

2. Start each exercise at ♩ = 160. *You* decide when you will change to two pulses per measure.

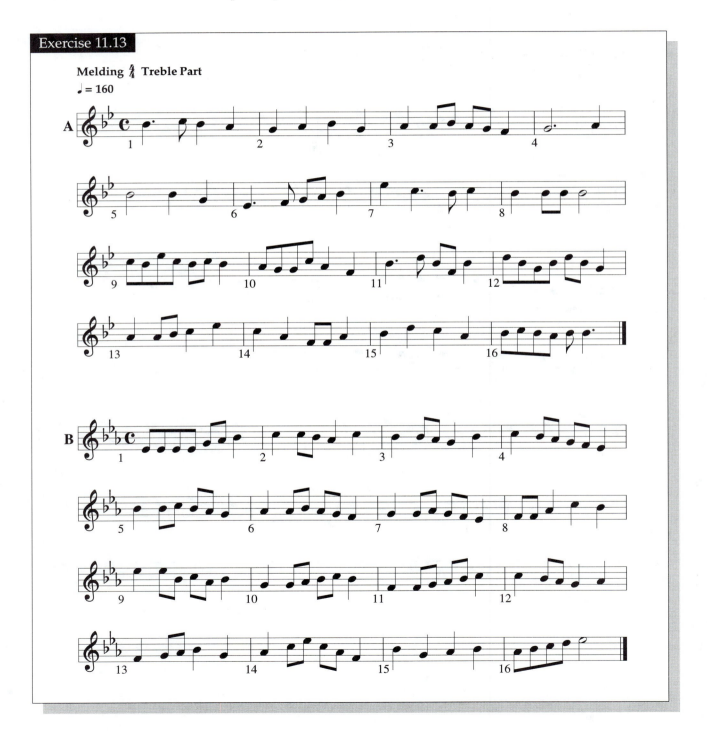

Exercise 11.13

Exercise 11.13

Melding $\frac{4}{4}$ F Part

♩ = 160

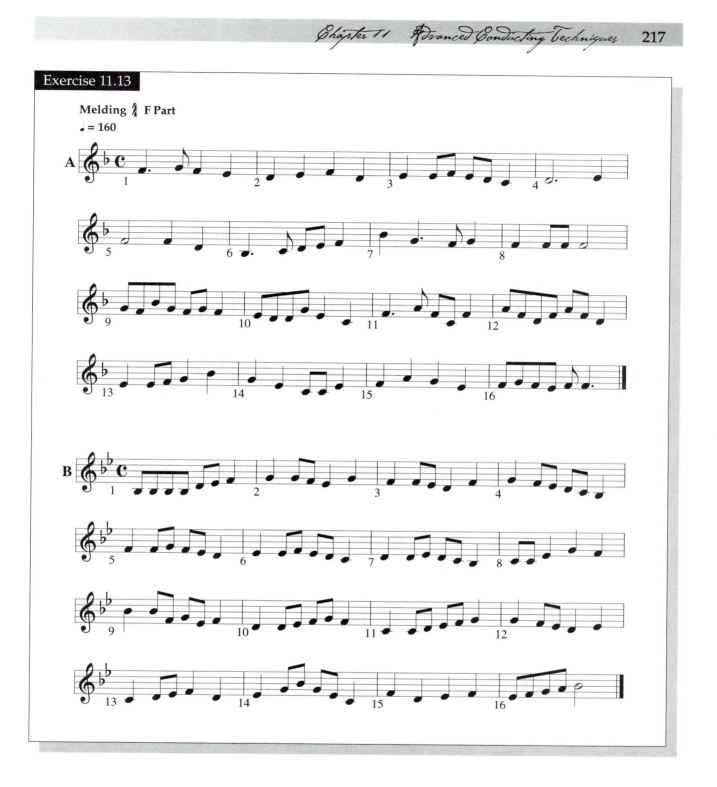

Exercise 11.13

Melding $\frac{4}{4}$ **E♭ Part**

$\quad$ ♩ = 160

Exercise 11.13

Melding $\frac{4}{4}$ Bb Part

♩ = 160

Exercise 11.13

Melding $\frac{4}{4}$ **Bass Part**

$\quad \downarrow = 160$

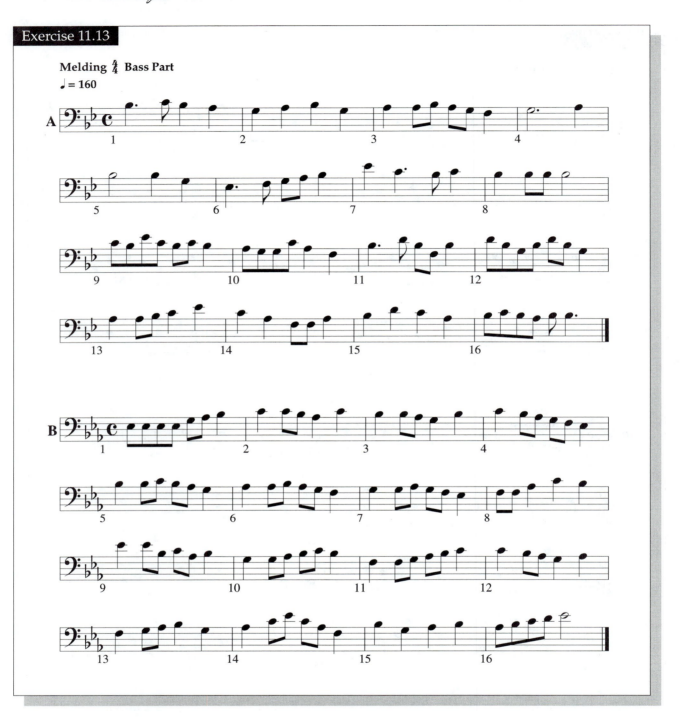

Melding in Slow Tempo ¾ Time

1. Use a slow melding pattern.

2. Vary tempo markings (♩ = 60).

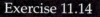

Exercise 11.14

Melding in a Slow Tempo $\frac{3}{4}$

E♭ Part

♩ = 60

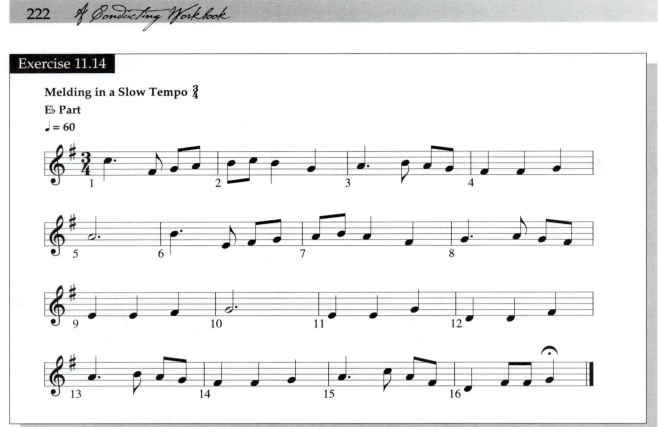

Exercise 11.14

Melding in a Slow Tempo $\frac{3}{4}$

B♭ Part

♩ = 60

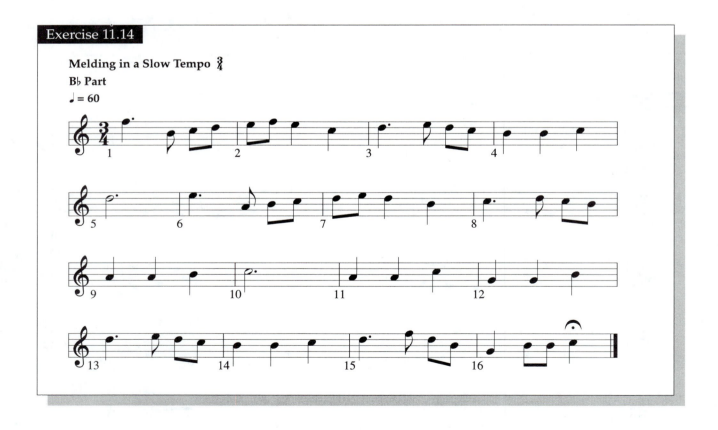

Exercise 11.14

Melding in a Slow Tempo $\frac{3}{4}$
Bass Part

Melding in Slow Tempo $\frac{4}{4}$ Time

Exercise 11.15

1. Use a slow melding pattern.
2. Vary tempo markings ($\quarternote = 60$).

Exercise 11.15

Melding in a Slow Tempo $\frac{4}{4}$
Treble Part

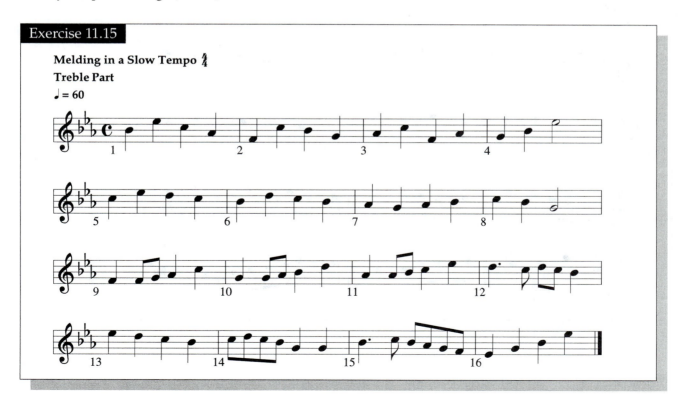

Exercise 11.15

Melding in a Slow Tempo 4/4

F Part

♩ = 60

Exercise 11.15

Melding in a Slow Tempo 4/4

E♭ Part

♩ = 60

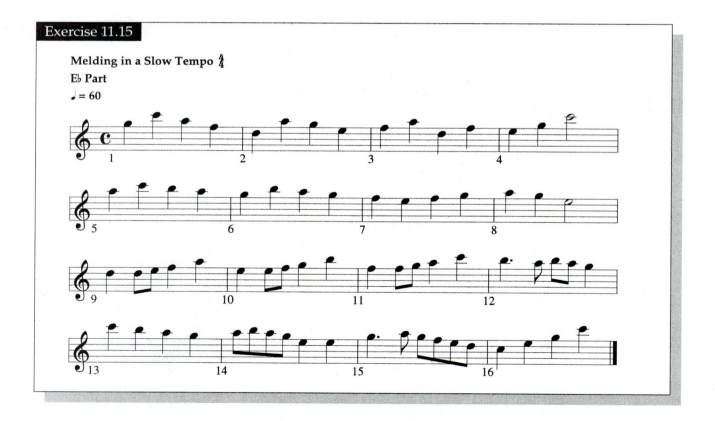

Exercise 11.15

Melding in a Slow Tempo $\frac{4}{4}$
Bb Part
♩ = 60

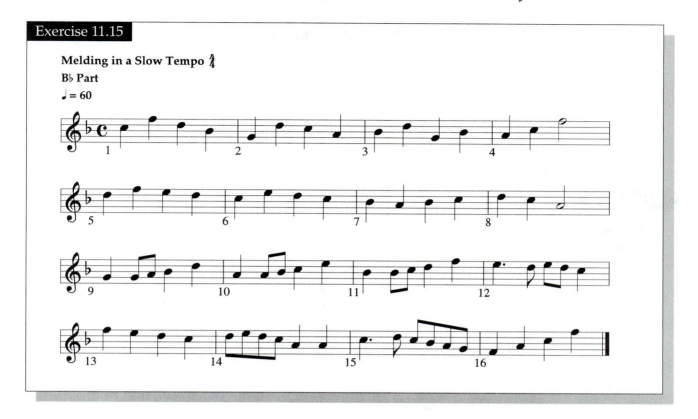

Exercise 11.15

Melding in a Slow Tempo $\frac{4}{4}$
Bass Part
♩ = 60

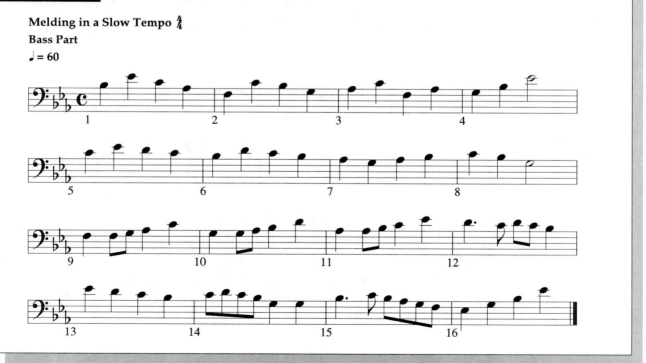

Exercise 11.16   Melding in Slow Tempo, Harmony

1. Use a melding pattern.

2. Vary tempo marking.

3. Select a part appropriate for your instrument and transpose if necessary (♩ = 60).

Exercise 11.16

Melding in a Slow Tempo Harmonized ¾

♩ = 60

Exercise 11.16

Melding in a Slow Tempo Harmonized $\frac{4}{4}$

$\quad$ = 60

Appendices

Effective Organizational Techniques

*S*ome type of systematic organization should be used for the effective distribution of concert and marching band music. If a system is in place, music can be distributed quickly, and if misplaced it can easily be returned to the musician. While each situation is different and each conductor will need to use a distribution system tailored to his or her individual needs, here are two possibilities.

1. In concert ensemble, number each folder and each piece of music before placing it in the folder. See Chart A for concert ensemble.

Folder	Instrument	Folder	Instrument
1	Flute I	27	Cornet II
2	Flute II	28	Cornet III
3	Oboe I	29	Flugelhorn I
4	Oboe II	30	Flugelhorn II
5	English Horn	31	Horn I
6	Bassoon I	32	Horn II
7	Bassoon II	33	Horn III
8	Contra Bassoon	34	Horn IV
9	E♭ Soprano Clarinet	35	Trombone I
10	Clarinet I	36	Trombone II
11	Clarinet II	37	Trombone III
12	Clarinet III	38	Bass Trombone
13	Alto Clarinet	39	Euphonium B.C.
14	Bass Clarinet	40	Euphonium T.C.
15	Contra Alto Clarinet	41	Baritone B.C.
16	Contra Bass Clarinet	42	Baritone T.C.
17	Soprano Saxophone	43	Tuba/Sousaphone I
18	Alto Saxophone I	44	Tuba/Sousaphone II
19	Alto Saxophone II	45	String Bass
20	Tenor Saxophone I	46	Timpani
21	Tenor Saxophone II	47	Keyboard Percussion
22	Baritone Saxophone	48	Auxiliary Percussion
23	Trumpet I	49	Percussion I
24	Trumpet II	50	Percussion II
25	Trumpet III	51	Harp
26	Cornet I	52	Piano

Chart A.
Concert Ensemble
Numbering System

2. In marching band, assign each musician a place in a block band form. Designating each marcher by rank and file works for any size marching band. See Chart B for marching band.

Chart B.
Marching
Band

File 6	File 5	File 4	File 3	File 2	File 1	
Trb II #16 Junior Mary Jane	Trb. II #15 Sophomore C. Jones	Trb.II #14 Senior Marie T.	Trb.I #13 Freshman Bob Adams	Trb. I #12 Freshman Margo Lee	Trb. I #11 Senior Will Huff	**Rank 1**
#26	#25	#24	#23	#22	Sax I #21 Senior Ralph M.	**Rank 2**
#36	#35	#34	#33	#32	#31	**Rank 3**
#46	#45	#44	#43	#42	#41	**Rank 4**
#56	#55	#54	Snare #53 Sophomore Bill Green	#52	#51	**Rank 5**
#66	#65	#64	#63	#62	#61	**Rank 6**
#76	#75	#74	#73	#72	#71	**Rank 7**

Rank 1, File 1, identifies player 11, Will Huff, a senior playing first trombone parts. Number 53 identifies Bill Green, a sophomore playing snare drum in Rank 5, File 3. Put each student's number on each piece of music in his or her numbered folder. Expanding the ranks and files will accommodate any size band.

Evaluations

The following form is useful for self-evaluation.

Self-Evaluation Form

Name (please print)
_____

Composition/exercise being conducted
_____

Student Grade _____ Professor Grade _____

Comments from you about your conducting and rationale for the grade you give yourself
_____

_____

_____

_____

_____

_____

_____

_____

_____

_____

_____

_____

_____

_____

_____

_____

_____

_____

_____

_____

At some point in the class, at the discretion of the instructor, members of the student ensemble may be asked to comment on the performance of each student conductor. Oral and/or written comments may be solicited (even a letter grade). Written comments are most valuable because they provide a record against which the student conductor can gauge performance and improvement.

The following form is included for use by the instructor and student evaluators if appropriate. You are encouraged to copy this form as needed— or you may want to generate your own forms and grading system.

Conductor Evaluation Form

Student conductor _____

Exercise/composition _____

1. Energy level   ☐ too little   ☐ too much   ☐ appropriate

2. Accuracy of pattern   ☐ accurate   ☐ lacks clarity   ☐ too flowery

3. Ictus   ☐ accurate   ☐ indefinite   ☐ misplaced

4. Takt   ☐ even ictus to ictus   ☐ unnecessary or out of pattern movement

5. Rebound   ☐ too short   ☐ too long   ☐ matches style of ictus

6. Posture   ☐ leaning too far forward   ☐ leaning too far back   ☐ leaning to the right   ☐ leaning to the left

7. Position of arms   ☐ too far back   ☐ too extended   ☐ too stiff   ☐ moving from shoulder
☐ moving from elbow   ☐ too close to body

8. Confidence   ☐ looks at ease   ☐ looks awkward   ☐ confident presentation

9. Appearance   ☐ well groomed   ☐ appropriate dress   ☐ inappropriate dress

10. Placement of feet   ☐ weight on both feet   ☐ right foot   ☐ left foot

11. Facial expression   ☐ pleasant   ☐ worried   ☐ grim   ☐ panic   ☐ happy

12. Conductor is   ☐ conducting the group   ☐ following the group

13. Eye contact   ☐ excellent   ☐ good   ☐ average   ☐ poor

14. Releases   ☐ in appropriate direction   ☐ consistent with style, dynamics, and pattern

15. Baton   ☐ grip   ☐ extension of wrist   ☐ forearm position

16. Cues   ☐ early   ☐ on time   ☐ late   ☐ lacks clarity

17. Right wrist   ☐ comfortable   ☐ too stiff   ☐ too floppy

18. Left arm   ☐ comfortable   ☐ coordination awkward

19. Stability of pattern   ☐ steady   ☐ tempo gets faster   ☐ tempo gets slower   ☐ tempo wanders

20. Imposition of will   ☐ extroverted   ☐ demanding   ☐ forceful   ☐ introverted   ☐ lethargic

21. Imposition of musicality   ☐ extroverted   ☐ demanding   ☐ forceful

Grade _____   Evaluator _____